THE TEXAS CHRONICLES

THE HISTORY OF TEXAS
FROM EARLIEST TIMES TO THE PRESENT DAY

With grateful thanks to our partner:

"If we don't know where we've been,
we sure don't know where we're going."

Lt. Governor Bob Bullock (1929–1999)

Thanks also to:

Texas State Historical Association
Texas State Library and Archives Commission
Texas Historical Commission
Space Center Houston
LBJ Presidential Library
Rosenberg Library
NASA

First published in 2019 by What on Earth Books

Written by Mark Skipworth. Created by Christopher Lloyd. Additional
research by Julie Deegan. Edited by Ali Glossop. Design by Assunção
Sampayo and Andy Forshaw, based on series design by Grade Design.
Picture research by Felicity Page. Editorial contributions and thanks to:
Kate Betz; Randolph B. Campbell; Ryan Schumacher; Jelain Chubb;
Richard Gilreath; Tonia Wood; Chris Florance; Steve Cure; Marianne
Dyson; Dave Williams; Pat Hardy; Roger Louis; and Walter Buenger.

Library of Congress Cataloging-in-Publication Data available
upon request

ISBN: 978-1-9998028-7-5

Printed in China

2 4 6 8 10 9 7 5 3 1

whatonearthbooks.com

THE TEXAS CHRONICLES

CABEZA DE VACA

ESTEVANICO

A WORLD BEYOND IMAGINATION

By our special envoy in Mexico City
August 1, 1536

BY order of his Catholic Majesty, Charles, Holy Roman Emperor and King of Spain, we thank God for the miraculous return of a daring Spanish explorer who survived an ordeal lasting nearly eight years—including a 2,400-mile trek on foot across the northern wilderness of New Spain in the Americas.

Álvar Núñez Cabeza de Vaca spent many of those years living with native peoples before escaping to freedom with three companions. His remarkable story is one of the first accounts of this vast land and its inhabitants. In a world beyond imagination, he came upon many native peoples with very different customs from our own.

Cabeza de Vaca joined Spain's Narváez Expedition to the Gulf Coast region. Members of the expedition later became separated while traveling along the coastline by raft. It is our opinion that this is the same coastline explorer Alonso Álvarez de Pineda saw and mapped in 1519, although he did not set foot on its shores.

Hungry and weak from sickness, Cabeza de Vaca and a party of men were washed ashore on an island he will name the "Isle of Misfortune." The native people there turned out to be kind, bringing the survivors fish to eat, and weeping with grief when some of them died. Native people became upset when they learned that some starving survivors resorted to eating the bodies of their fellow explorers who had died.

Cabeza de Vaca observed many of the customs of these Native Americans. He was asked to treat sick people, in return for food. Some survivors managed to leave, but he was unable to join them because of illness. He became a merchant trading in seashells.

BEFORE the arrival of Europeans, the land that would become Texas had been home to Native American peoples for thousands of years. Some lived in cities and villages; others were migratory. They farmed, hunted, and developed trade routes across the land. Their artifacts are evidence of complex cultures.

He eventually got away and rejoined some of his fellow explorers. One of them was named Estevanico, an enslaved man from Africa.

The explorers were held captive by another group of native people. According to Cabeza de Vaca, these people believed in the power of dreams. They struggled to feed themselves, eating spiders, worms, and snakes when other foods were scarce. He also tells of strange black and brown cows that sometimes appeared, with long fur and small horns, and claims to have seen evidence of gold.

Cabeza de Vaca made his escape with Estevanico and two other companions while their captors were harvesting prickly pears. The four "ragged castaways" spent about two years trekking across the northern wilderness before meeting fellow Spanish people, and finally made their way south to Mexico City. He plans to give a full account of his incredible adventure in a book he wants to write.

We pray that other explorers will follow his example and embark on future expeditions to explore these new lands, and spread the Word of God.

DOOMED FRENCH COLONY

Royal road is lifeline for missions

By our missionary brother in San Antonio
January 1, 1722

By our dispatch writer on Matagorda Bay
April 23, 1689

IN honor of your Excellency, Viceroy of New Spain, I am commanded by Alonso de Léon, leader of our expedition and governor of Coahuila, to report the discovery of the French colony founded by René Robert Cavelier, Sieur de La Salle.

Guided by a survivor of La Salle's settlement, our party of 114 men yesterday came upon the colony in the area of Matagorda Bay, along the southern coast of Tejas. I am pleased to inform you that it is no more.

All that remains is a ghost town. We found six dwellings built from poles plastered with mud and roofs made with bison hides. We came across another building where pigs had been fattened. The settlement is a bone-chilling scene of desolation.

Among the ruins, we discovered three bodies and eight cannons. Our priest, Father Massanet, has performed burial rites for the deceased.

La Salle's colony is no longer a threat to our shipping, but we cannot be certain that its failure is the end of French ambitions. Let me remind you that La Salle was a great explorer, claiming all the lands drained by the Mississippi River for France and naming the region "Louisiana" in honor of French King Louis XIV. It is said that he raised the French coat of arms, the fleur-de-lis, at the settlement, despite our Spanish claim to the territory.

We are starting to piece together the gruesome fate of La Salle and his colony of about 200 settlers. It seems he was attempting to establish a settlement near the Mississippi, but his ships lost their way, and landed instead at Matagorda Bay. We know that two of the ships were destroyed, as an earlier expedition found the wreck of *La Belle* and pieces of *L'Aimable*. Searching for the Mississippi, La Salle and a party of men walked in the wrong direction all the way to the Rio Grande and back.

Two years after their arrival, less than a quarter of the settlers remained alive. Many had perished from sickness, snake bites, or attacks by native peoples. Some even deserted to live with friendly Caddo groups.

La Salle's desperate survival plan was to travel thousands of miles overland to Canada. He set off with a second small party but was shot and killed, betrayed in an ambush following a dispute among his own countrymen.

This unhappy episode came to a violent end when the remaining colonists were massacred by the Karankawa people, who, it is said, were provoked after the French stole a canoe. The children survived, and, it is believed, were adopted into their group. May God protect them!

TO all our Catholic faithful, and their communities, greetings! We celebrate the New Year with great hopes for the missions, the Camino Real de los Tejas, and Tejas' future in New Spain.

The Camino Real, a network of trails, is sometimes no more than a mule track but, nonetheless, has special status as the "King's Highway." From the Rio Grande to the Red River, it is helping us reach native peoples with our important missionary work, and God willing, convert them to Christianity.

Established last century, it connects our missions and military garrisons, or presidios, including the new Mission San José in San Antonio, and extends north to Nacogdoches and beyond. It provides a lifeline for the Franciscans—members of a Christian religious order—who run the missions and are using it to obtain supplies.

With links to the government center of Mexico City, the Camino Real is helping to control the territory. No foreign state can now challenge Spain's claim to Tejas—least of all, France.

SPANISH explorer, or conquistador, Luis de Moscoso Alvarado, made contact with the Caddo people in the 1540s. The Spanish turned "techas," the Caddo word for "friends," into "Tejas," and used it to describe the territory's many native peoples. The name later changed to "Texas," and the state motto today celebrates the original meaning—"Friendship."

SPANISH CLASH WITH NEW POWER—THE COMANCHES

By our military envoy in the Presidio de San Sabá
March 19, 1758

IT is my sad duty to report that our largest Catholic mission in the area has been destroyed by the fearsome Comanche people and their allies. The mission was burned down, and eight inhabitants, including two priests, were killed.

At least 2,000 Comanches, helped by the Wichitas and other native warriors, attacked the Santa Cruz de San Sabá Mission. It was established by Franciscans only about a year ago to convert the Apache people to Christianity.

Painted black and red, and armed with muskets and bows, the Comanches surrounded the mission, eventually setting fire to its wooden stockade. All except one of our riders sent to protect the mission were slaughtered. The rest of us were trapped here inside the presidio three miles away. The body of a priest was later found in the mission chapel, where he had remained at prayer.

We have learned that the Comanches are mortal enemies of the Apaches whom they suspect are allied with us, the Spanish. This may explain the ferocious attack on our mission. The Comanches have now moved on, but they may well return.

They are a formidable fighting force capable of threatening our control of Texas. We first became aware of them after their migration south across the Red River in pursuit of bison—also called buffalo—and mustangs. They appeared only in family groups or small bands . . . until now.

The Comanches acquired horses in the last century and are exceptional riders, giving them great advantage in hunting and warfare. Their children learn to ride at an early age, and their women riders are as skilled as the men.

The word "Comanche" is from the Ute people, and means "enemy," but the Comanches call themselves "Numunuu"—"The People."

Each Comanche group has both a "peace" chief and a "war" chief. These leaders are chosen by common consent. But individuals have great freedoms within a group and often do not appear bound by the decisions of their councils of chiefs.

The Comanches are migratory, following the bison herds. The people rely on the animals as a vital source of food and use their hides to make clothing, shelter, and other essentials. They use every piece of the bison to support their lives. The Comanches also trade bison products and horses with the Wichitas and the French. In return, they receive other foods and goods, including firearms.

We fear their empire, known as the "Comanchería," will dominate the Southern Plains. This could bring further conflict with native peoples, especially the Apaches, as well as with our own inhabitants in New Spain.

Spanish soldiers out on expeditions have been instructed to return to their presidios to protect our Catholic missions from possible further attack. It may be necessary to move other settlers south to San Antonio.

IN 1759, seeking to punish the attackers of San Sabá Mission, a Spanish force of about 600 men challenged the Wichitas on the Red River, but were forced to retreat. Native peoples in northern Texas formed a stronger force than the Spanish themselves. San Sabá Mission was never rebuilt, but a painting, above, was commissioned to honor the priests' martyrdom.

PIRATES SLAUGHTER NATIVE ISLAND PEOPLE

FRENCH pirate Jean Laffite and his men are said to have dealt a blow to a once-powerful native people, a defeat from which the group may never recover, *writes our news correspondent, on March 1, 1821.*

Stories are circulating that at least 300 Karankawa warriors attacked the lawless smuggler's base, named "Campeche," on Galveston Island, after Laffite's men kidnapped a Karankawa woman.

But their bows and arrows were overpowered by the guns and cannons of Laffite's force of 200 men. The Karankawas stood no chance.

The wily buccaneer soon triumphed after his men killed or wounded many native people. Their defeat is likely to be the beginning of the end for the badly weakened Karankawas who will struggle to stop future settlers from entering the Gulf Coast territory.

The Karankawas' relations with the pirates have been good until this time.

Laffite set up his smuggler's base four years ago, requiring newcomers to swear loyalty to him. He claims the U.S. is his adopted country. (The portrait, right, is said to be of him despite the clothing not being typical of the time.)

By our news correspondent
December 15, 1821

AUSTIN FOUNDS THE FIRST ANGLO COLONY

BY land and sea, the first settlers of a new Anglo colony have begun to arrive in Mexican Texas, an event that marks the start of a new era of colonization in the territory.

About 300 Anglo families or partnerships are being allowed to settle between the Colorado and Brazos Rivers. The colony has been founded by land agent, or empresario, Stephen F. Austin. He was able to set up the colony after his father, Moses, was granted land there before he died.

Earlier this year, Mexico took control of Texas after winning its independence from Spain. Austin hopes the Mexican authorities will view the colonists as a boost to the Texas economy and that they will help deter raids by native peoples.

Anglos are settling in the remote territory after the authorities struggled to persuade enough of its citizens to move there.

There has been no shortage of Anglo families eager to take up the offer of cheap Texas land after a long economic downturn and the increased cost of U.S. land.

The Anglo settlers are bringing enslaved people to work the land, and are required to become Mexican citizens, learn Spanish, and adopt the Catholic faith. Irish people are also among the earliest settlers. Other empresarios are expected to follow.

Meanwhile, with the ending of Spanish control, some Americans have quietly settled in eastern Texas, near Nacogdoches, without permission from the new Mexican government.

Austin is not expecting the Mexican authorities to protect his colonists. One idea is to create a unit of "rangers for the common defense" to help protect his colonists against the threat of raids by native peoples.

For his services, Austin will receive 12.5 cents an acre, paid to him by each family of colonists. He may also receive land from the Mexican government.

Austin is already being called the "Father of Texas" by many Anglo settlers.

MARTÍN DE LÉON became Texas' second empresario and was the only Mexican-born man to create a colony. In 1824, he founded Guadalupe Victoria, later renamed Victoria. Under Spanish laws protecting women's property rights, De Léon's widow, Patricia de la Garza, managed their ranch, and expanded it.

MEXICAN RULERS ALLOW TEXAS SLAVERY

SLAVERY can legally continue in Mexican Texas despite being banned elsewhere in the Republic of Mexico, its citizens were told yesterday, *writes our politics editor, December 3, 1829.*

To the relief of many Anglo settlers, a decree to abolish slavery in the Mexican republic will not be enforced in Texas, one of its northern territories.

It follows warnings by Stephen F. Austin that without slave labor, Texas will not have enough workers to farm rich cotton plantations.

Vicente Ramón Guerrero, pictured left, president of Mexico and a former leader of Mexico's rebellion against Spain, issued the decree in September. Mexican-born Guerrero, who is said to have some African heritage, is a strong campaigner against the evils of slavery.

The decree alarmed Texas slave owners, who said that freeing enslaved people amounted to stealing their property. Leaders of the Tejanos—Texas-born people of Hispanic background—have helped Texas' slave-owning settlers. They allowed enslaved people to enter the territory under a system of "indentured servitude," that has been said to be slavery in all but name.

Despite the decree not being enforced, many slave-owning settlers in Texas believe their interests are no longer safe under the Mexican republic.

ALAMO DISASTER!

BRAVE DEFENDERS WILL GO INTO LEGEND

By our war correspondent
March 7, 1836

THE defenders of the Alamo yesterday claimed their place in history after sacrificing their lives in the struggle for Texas independence. Texians have been making a stand against Antonio López de Santa Anna after he established himself as military dictator of Mexico, including its northern territory of Texas.

Against overwhelming Mexican forces, 189 defenders of the San Antonio stronghold died in battle, or were executed, and their bodies burned. They included commander William B. Travis, pictured middle above, frontiersman David Crockett, left, and famed adventurer James Bowie, right, who died on his sick bed, riddled with bullets. The few who survived included several women, children, and an enslaved man named Joe.

The 13-day siege ended after a dawn attack by hundreds of Mexican troops who stormed the Alamo. A former Catholic mission that later served as a Spanish military garrison, it was chosen as a base by Texians for its position, giving them time to alert Anglo and Tejano settlements of a Mexican advance.

Days before the siege, Bowie had arrived on the orders of Sam Houston, commander of the Texas forces. Although a slave trader and drunk, Bowie had shown himself to be an inspiring leader in the early days of the Texas Revolution.

He was joined by Travis, who raised a company of just 30 men and agreed to share command with Bowie. Crockett, who had left his Tennessee home for a new life in Texas, brought a small band of American volunteers.

Santa Anna and his men arrived at the Alamo late last month. Proclaiming himself "Napoleon of the West," he was determined to restore Mexican control. To make clear his intentions, Santa Anna hoisted a red flag to signify no mercy.

The Mexicans surrounded the fort and began bombarding it. Bowie became sick, and Travis took full command, issuing a plea for help to the "People of Texas and All Americans in the World," and declaring that he would "never surrender or retreat," and that the choice before the defenders was "Victory or Death."

Crossing Mexican lines, 32 troops arrived to fight—and die. Travis' inspiring words will be remembered for generations to come.

With hopes of relief fading, Travis called his command together. The story goes that he drew a line in the dirt with his sword, and asked that everyone willing to die for freedom step across it—but we may never know what really happened. The fighting was ferocious, as Travis' force defended the Alamo. Mexican troops also fought bravely, and the battle left about 600 of them killed or wounded.

The survival of Texas hangs in the balance. Unless Santa Anna is defeated, the Anglos—and many Tejanos—could be swept away.

Massacre at Goliad fort

TREACHERY! At least 340 men fighting for Texas independence were executed yesterday after surrendering to Santa Anna's Mexican forces, *writes our war correspondent, March 28, 1836.*

The people of Texas have been fleeing their homes in panic after the Alamo's fall. Col. James F. Fannin and his men confronted Mexican forces at the Battle of Coleto, but they surrendered on condition the Mexicans treated them as prisoners of war.

About 240 of Fannin's men were marched back to their fort at Goliad and imprisoned inside the former Spanish presidio. About 50 more, including the wounded and some doctors, were delivered to the mission days later. About 80 men of the Georgia Battalion—volunteers from the U.S. who had surrendered to Santa Anna in a separate battle—also arrived.

Santa Anna ordered the execution of these "foreigners." The men were marched out, believing they were to gather wood or drive cattle. Some even sang "Home Sweet Home" the night before their deaths. Firing squads gunned down many, and others were killed by bayonet or lance. The wounded including Fannin were executed inside the presidio, and their bodies were burned.

Twenty-eight escaped the firing squads, and 20 more survived largely because of Francita Alavez, hailed the "Angel of Goliad" and heroine of the Texas Revolution. She hid away some of them before the massacre and pleaded for others to be spared.

This massacre has further enraged the people of Texas, and the U.S. These are dark days, but Santa Anna is likely to pay a high price for his infamous cruelty.

JOANNA TROUTMAN made a flag for Georgia volunteers fighting in the Texas Revolution. It had a blue star on a white background and the words "Liberty or Death." Nearly all the Georgians died in the Goliad Massacre, but Troutman's flag may have been inspiration for the Lone Star Flag, later adopted by the Republic of Texas.

VICTORY AT SAN JACINTO

TEXAS WINS INDEPENDENCE AFTER DEFEAT OF SANTA ANNA'S FORCES

By our war correspondent
April 22, 1836

TEXAS gained its independence in spectacular fashion yesterday when Sam Houston's men inflicted a crushing defeat on Santa Anna's army at the Battle of San Jacinto. The Mexican dictator, who disappeared during the conflict, was captured today after a search party found him hiding in the grass.

According to witnesses, Santa Anna's army was taken by surprise. The battle lasted less than 20 minutes. A Texas force of about 900 performed a near miracle by killing 630 Mexicans and taking 730 prisoner. Only nine of Houston's men were killed.

This glorious victory is a personal triumph for Houston, pictured above as an older man, commander-in-chief of the Texas army, who showed courage after his ankle was shattered by a musket ball. He has silenced criticism from fellow revolutionary leaders of his previous retreats.

Days earlier, Santa Anna moved against the Texas government at New Washington, but its members had fled. The situation could not have looked bleaker for the revolutionaries.

Houston's men received a boost when the "Twin Sisters" arrived—a gift of two cannon from the people of the U.S. state of Ohio, who raised funds to aid Texas independence.

Houston decided to attack Santa Anna's army near the San Jacinto River. He placed his men in battle formation while Mexican troops were resting. Mexican lookouts failed to detect them until it was too late. Houston's line of troops charged the Mexican camp with the battle cry, "Remember the Alamo! Remember Goliad!" Tejanos led by Juan N. Seguín joined the Texas line.

Santa Anna disappeared during the battle. Search parties sent out this morning found him hiding in the grass, dirty and wet. None of them recognized him until he was addressed as "El Presidente" by other Mexican prisoners.

Houston has rejected demands for Santa Anna's execution. By keeping him as a prisoner, he believes the Mexican dictator has no choice but to order withdrawal of his troops. The Republic of Texas begins.

> MEXICO refused to recognize Texas independence, despite Santa Anna's defeat. It invaded the new republic in 1842. Seeking revenge, Texian Col. William S. Fisher led the Mier Expedition into Mexico. The raid failed disastrously, and his men surrendered. Santa Anna ordered one in 10 executed, and forced the prisoners to draw lots to decide who would die.

EBERLY IS HERO OF THE ARCHIVES WAR

AUSTIN has been saved as capital of the Republic of Texas after an attempt to remove its government archives was dramatically thwarted, *writes our politics correspondent, January 2, 1843.*

The records were returned to the city yesterday, thanks to the quick thinking of local innkeeper Angelina Eberly and the bravery of local citizens.

Sam Houston, re-elected president of the republic, had waged a campaign to have the archives moved from Austin, arguing that the capital is a vulnerable location—open to attack by Comanches and other Native American groups, as well as Mexicans who refuse to recognize Texas independence.

Eberly spotted about 20 men loading the archives into wagons on Houston's orders, and raced to the town cannon. She fired, blowing a hole in the Texas General Land Office building, alerting the locals who chased down the men.

The "Archives War" is the climax of rivalry between Houston and the previous president, Mirabeau B. Lamar, who moved the young republic's capital to Austin, named for Stephen F. Austin, the first Anglo colonist.

By our politics editor
December 30, 1845

CITIZENS CELEBRATE BIRTH OF 28TH STATE

THE people of Texas awoke today to find themselves citizens of the 28th State of the Union after voters in the republic approved its takeover by the United States.

A statehood ceremony will celebrate the historic event, declaring "the Republic of Texas is no more." This brings independent Texas to an end nearly ten years after it was created, at the cost of many lives in the revolution against Mexico.

Numerous states were U.S. territories before joining the Union, but Texas is an independent country. Unlike many annexations in history, however, the U.S. takeover has been welcomed by the republic's citizens.

Texas' entry into the Union is in large part due to U.S. President James K. Polk, champion of the idea called "Manifest Destiny"—that it is inevitable and desirable that the U.S. expands to include all lands from the Atlantic Coast to the Pacific Ocean.

A new state constitution, modeled on those of southern states, gives all white males the vote and also continues slavery. James Pinckney Henderson, a former Texas representative to Britain and France, has been elected first governor of Texas. A Senate and a House of Representatives will form the state legislature.

The Lone Star Flag—the national flag of the republic approved by former Texas President Lamar in 1839—will become the state flag. It will be only a matter of time before the new state comes to be known as the "Lone Star State."

Statehood is a victory for campaigners such as Sam Houston, former president of Texas. They made several attempts to be annexed by the U.S., which had proved unsuccessful—until now.

Others in Texas are less enthusiastic about the republic's admission to the Union, wanting it to remain an independent nation. Anti-slavery citizens in the U.S. have also voiced opposition because the new state will continue to allow slavery.

Those who voted for annexation, however, are looking forward to the greater security the U.S. will bring as the state's chief protector.

Future settlers from North America and Europe will also feel reassured that Texas will be a safe new home.

Expanding the cotton industry is certain to result in a big increase in the number of enslaved people working the land, while the growth of cattle ranching is creating a new generation of "cowboys." These men gained many of their riding and roping skills from the early Spanish "vaqueros."

Yet the prospect of conflict with Mexico remains. The U.S. wants to define the border between Texas and Mexico at the Rio Grande, but Mexico already objects.

Founding of German Texas

GERMAN prince Carl of Solms-Braunfels established New Braunfels, a German colony in Texas. Other settlements followed, including Fredericksburg, whose founder, John O. Meusebach, encouraged German immigrants and Comanches to live peacefully side by side. A treaty of 1847 allowed settlers and Native American people, pictured right, to go unharmed into each other's territory. It was one of the few pacts between settlers and Native Americans that both parties honored.

WAR ENDS BORDER DISPUTE

TEXANS yesterday celebrated a peace treaty that makes the Rio Grande the official border with Mexico, *writes our defense editor, February 3, 1848*. The U.S. claimed victory in the U.S.–Mexican War after American troops captured Mexico City, the Mexican capital.

The Treaty of Guadalupe Hidalgo has ended the war, which began with the U.S. annexation of Texas in 1845. It lays to rest years of dispute about the border.

The U.S. had defined the Rio Grande as the border, but Mexico insisted it was the Nueces River. When the Mexicans spotted American troops along the Rio Grande's north bank, Mexico saw their presence as an act of war.

The Battle of Palo Alto near Brownsville was the first major conflict. U.S. troops then invaded Mexico by land and sea, helped by Texas Rangers who were nicknamed "Los Diablos Tejanos" for their ruthless fighting spirit. American success sent Mexican leader Santa Anna into exile.

Mexico has finally given up its claim to Texas and in return for about $18 million, the U.S. has acquired its vast northern territories, including California, Nevada, and Utah.

TEXAS JOINS CONFEDERACY

CIVIL WAR LOOMS AS STATE SPLITS FROM THE UNION TO KEEP SLAVERY

By our politics editor
March 17, 1861

TEXAS has become part of the Confederate States of America, and a bloody civil war between the North and South now looks inevitable.

In an earlier statewide referendum, Texas citizens approved a declaration to break away from the Union in defense of slavery. As the news spread across the state, many celebrated wildly, hoisting the Lone Star Flag where the national flag once flew. But the U.S. government refuses to recognize Texas' and other slave states' decision to leave.

The split follows the election of U.S. President Abraham Lincoln who opposes slavery. Many southern states, including Texas, fear that slavery—on which their economies are built—will be abolished. Texas has joined

South Carolina, Mississippi, Florida, Alabama, Georgia, and Louisiana in breaking away from the Union, and other states may follow. One Texan is reported to have said: "The South without slavery would not be worth a mess of pottage [soup]."

Sam Houston, Texas governor and former president of the Republic of Texas, has warned of the terrible cost of a civil war. Although himself a slave owner, he predicts a war will

result in victory for the northern states and destruction of the South. He has been deposed as governor after refusing to take an oath of loyalty to the Confederacy. "I love Texas too well to bring civil strife and bloodshed upon her," he said.

The Lone Star State is today a major cotton producer, with a plantation system that relies on enslaved labor to farm the land. African Americans comprise nearly a third of the population—most are enslaved. Cotton is seen as a lifeline for the Confederacy, as it could be sold overseas to pay for weapons and food.

Some white farmers are afraid that, if emancipated, African Americans may take revenge and riot against their former masters. The Confederate states are prepared to take up arms to keep slavery alive and defend the soil and people of their homelands. But the future has never looked more uncertain.

LAST LAND BATTLE OF THE CIVIL WAR FOUGHT IN TEXAS

By our war correspondent
May 14, 1865

TEXAS troops won the last land battle of the Civil War yesterday—for the Confederacy. But the victory at Palmito Ranch is too little, too late: the Civil War is over, the Confederacy already defeated, and the South devastated by conflict.

Texans triumphed after charging Union forces in a four-hour battle near Brownsville. Courageous fighting by the Union's 62nd Colored Infantry allowed most of the Union troops to escape.

The Texans, led by John Salmon "Rip" Ford, decided to fight in spite of the surrender of Confederate commander Robert E. Lee at Appomattox Court House and the fall of the Confederate capital, both in Virginia.

Rumors had already reached Union commanders that Confederate troops were still armed and ready to fight. About 17,000 Union troops—4,000 of them African American

IN 1862, Union forces, including four warships, took the port city of Galveston to prevent Texas from exporting and trading cotton in exchange for military supplies and weapons. The Confederacy retook Galveston in 1863, after a daring raid by the steamer ships *Bayou City* and the *Neptune*, which was sunk. A grounded Union ship was also blown up to prevent its capture by the Confederates.

infantry—prepared to invade Texas. But in reality, most war-weary Confederates had gone home.

Of 70,000 Texan Confederates who fought in the Civil War, many of those who survived will be able to look back with pride on a distinguished military record.

John Bell Hood's Texas Brigade gained one of the finest reputations after its part in many battles and skirmishes. The fighting force was so effective that Lee declared: "Texans always move them!" With other Confederate troops, the brigade surrendered at Appomattox, several weeks before the Battle of Palmito Ranch.

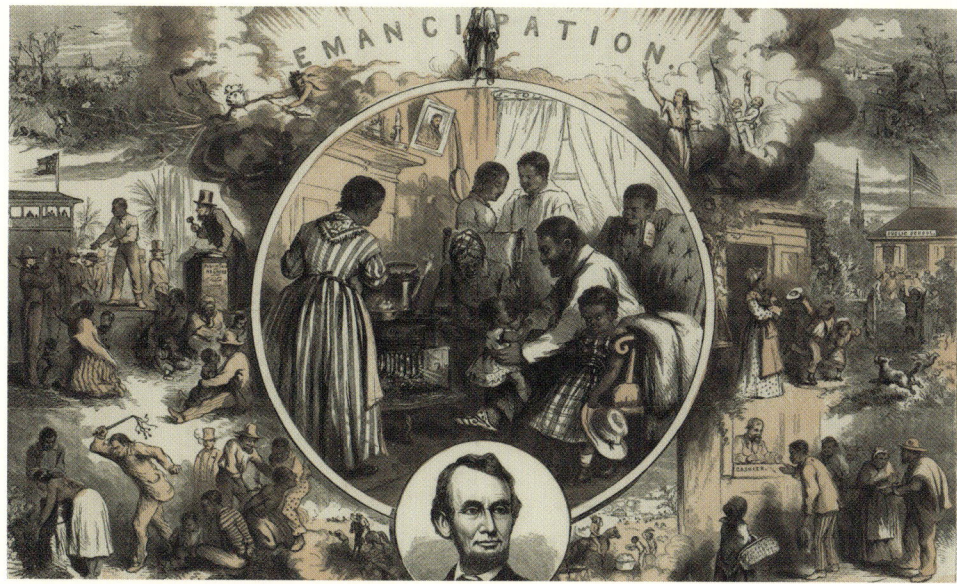

"JUNETEENTH" FREES ENSLAVED PEOPLE

By our civil rights correspondent
June 20, 1865

UNION general Gordon Granger made history yesterday when he declared the end of slavery for 250,000 African American men and women living in Texas.

With the Union defeat of the Confederacy, Granger arrived in the port city of Galveston and issued General Order Number 3. It reads: "The people of Texas are informed that, in accordance with a proclamation from the Executive of the United States, all slaves are free.

"This involves an absolute equality of personal rights and rights of property between former masters and slaves, and the connection heretofore existing between them becomes that between employer and hired labor.

"The freed are advised to remain at their present homes, and work for wages. They are informed that they will not be allowed to collect at military posts; and that they will not be supported in idleness either there or elsewhere."

The historic news follows the end of the Civil War, which claimed up to one million lives. It will be communicated by individual plantation owners to enslaved people over the coming weeks that they are freed from the evils of slavery.

AFTER the Civil War, enslaved people gained some basic rights under the 13th, 14th, and 15th Amendments to the U.S. Constitution. But "black codes" were introduced to weaken these gains, and by the 1890s, African Americans had to endure segregated public facilities. "Jim Crow" laws kept African American Texans apart from whites, and segregation also applied to Mexican Americans. Segregation existed in schools and most public places, including restaurants and theaters.

Granger's order comes more than two years after President Lincoln's Emancipation Proclamation, which declared all enslaved men and women in the "rebellious" southern states free.

Slave owners felt President Lincoln did not have authority over them, so they kept the news from enslaved people. The June 19, or "Juneteenth," order now requires slave owners to free them. Tragically, President Lincoln was assassinated in Washington, D.C., in April, and did not live to see this day.

Many of the freed will end up sharecroppers on their former masters' land or elsewhere. They will work to grow cotton and other crops, retaining a portion and giving the rest to the landowner.

But these farmers can expect a life of toil and poverty with little or no cash left over from their labors.

New State Police tackle wave of crime

THE Lone Star State is reaping the benefits of the Texas State Police, created last month by Governor Edmund J. Davis in a bid to curb widespread lawlessness, *writes our crime correspondent, August 31, 1870.*

In the aftermath of the Civil War, Texas has become a crime-ridden place with about 1,000 murders committed in three years, many of them by white people who have killed African Americans.

The force of about 200 has made many arrests—including for murder and attempted murder—in the first month alone.

Gangs of bandits are roaming along the Red River, and armed Ku Klux Klan white supremacy groups have sprung up.

The need for this statewide force to end the atrocities is obvious to all. Despite a promising start, the fact that the State Police includes African American officers is already making it unpopular. These officers face a huge challenge if they are to win the support of many white Texans.

The Reconstruction era is bringing about important changes after the Civil War. Texas is being readmitted to the Union after consenting to the 13th, 14th, and 15th Amendments to the U.S. Constitution, which taken together, abolish slavery, provide citizens with equal protection under the law, and give male citizens the vote, whatever their "race, color, or previous condition of servitude."

Said one young settler in Dallas: "The time will come when Texas Society will be the most refined of any in America.... But there is work to be done."

RAILROADS TO GROW THE STATE

THE first railroad to operate in Texas has finally been completed, nearly a decade after construction began, *writes our transport correspondent, October 1, 1860.* The Buffalo Bayou, Brazos and Colorado Railway Company now runs from Harrisburg to Alleyton, a distance of about 80 miles. But it has yet to reach the state capital of Austin, despite early plans.

The BBB & C was created by a group including Gen. Sidney Sherman, a leader of the Texas Revolution. It obtained a charter for the new railway company, and work began on the railroad in 1851. The first locomotive, named for Sherman, pictured right, arrived a year later.

The first 20 miles of track opened to great fanfare when the railroad went into service seven years ago. Many citizens cheered a new era in transportation that would boost industry and the growth of cities.

But Texas has been slow to embrace railroads. Financial backers elsewhere in the U.S. seem reluctant to invest in a frontier state, fearing raids by Native American peoples and bandits.

Thus, transportation remains a major problem facing Texas settlers. Roads are either non-existent or poor, and virtually impassable during wet weather. Many rivers are not deep enough for year-round transportation.

All this could change with the growth of railroads. Several

companies are already operating additional lines over short distances, mostly linking to sea or river ports in the Houston area.

The Lone Star State is slowly becoming connected. The first office for communication by telegraph opened in Texas in 1854.

ON THE CATTLE TRAIL

By our agriculture correspondent
June 30, 1879

ONE of the great migrations of livestock has been taking place in Texas. Cowboys are driving millions of cattle to market in the north and west of America.

The demand for beef to feed northern states after the Civil War has created a profitable trade. Cattle purchased for $2 in Texas sell for $20 in Kansas and nearly $50 at meat-packing plants beyond. This is a golden opportunity for ranchers in Texas, where cattle outnumber people.

Two of the most important cattle drives use the Chisholm Trail and the Fort Griffin–Dodge City Trail.

The Chisholm Trail is named after Scottish-Cherokee trader Jesse Chisholm, who hauled goods to Native American camps south of his Kansas trading post. Herder O. W. Wheeler and his partners later discovered Chisholm's wagon tracks and followed them to bring 2,400 steers into Indian Territory. The trail was later extended to Brownsville and the Rio Grande.

The drives start in early spring and can require a dozen or more cowboys to lead the difficult journeys, often across "Indian Country," which can last three to four months. The cowboys allow the livestock to spread out to graze, herding them at river crossings. According to cowboy wisdom, cattle that eat and drink their fill are unlikely to stampede.

Longhorns—a mix of Spanish stock and English cattle that Anglos are thought to have brought—are proving to be ideal trail cattle. One cowboy said it was an amazing sight to see— thousands of longhorns slowly making their way across the vast, open plains. One destination is the "cow town" of Abilene in Kansas, which is equipped with stockyards and has railroad connections north.

Lizzie E. Johnson, above, is one of the Texas "cattle queens." It has not been the custom for women to engage in business, but Johnson rounded up unbranded cattle roaming free after the Civil War, and has traveled the Chisholm Trail.

ONE of the youngest trail bosses was George Washington West, who secured a contract to deliver 14,000 cattle to a Native American reservation in Montana. The 19-year-old drove his herd from Lavaca County in Texas to the reservation, about 100 miles south of the Canadian border. It is probably the longest trail drive in history.

NATIVE AMERICANS' LAST STAND
COMANCHE WARRIORS FORCED TO SURRENDER TO U.S. ARMY

By our war correspondent
June 3, 1875

COMANCHE leader Quanah Parker and his band of warriors—the last great free-roaming Native American group in Texas—yesterday entered a U.S. Army post and surrendered.

Their defeat in the recent Red River War follows a military campaign by the U.S. Army to remove Native Americans from the Southern Plains and control them in reservations in Indian Territory. The warriors are to move to the Kiowa-Comanche reservation.

The Comanches' food supplies and way of life have been threatened ever since white hunters slaughtered millions of bison, which many Native Americans relied on for survival. Their surrender marks the end of an era for Parker and the nomadic peoples who followed the bison.

The Army previously tried to pacify Native American peoples by creating a frontier fort system, with limited success. The latest campaign, however, used army columns to crisscross the Texas Panhandle in an effort to locate and capture native groups. The groups tried to keep moving to avoid capture, but few had the strength or supplies to carry on.

Somehow, Parker's group of Comanches managed to keep going—until yesterday.

Federal agents have been impressed by the Comanche leader who, they say, possesses the qualities to become an influential spokesman for Native Americans as they adapt to reservation life.

Parker's father was the Comanche chief Peta Nocona, while his mother, Cynthia Ann Parker, pictured right, was an Illinois-born white woman who moved to Texas with her family. She was captured by Comanches as a young girl, and later married Peta Nocona.

When the group was attacked by Texas Rangers in 1860, Quanah

Parker took refuge among a Quahadi group, one of the most warlike Comanche bands. He became an expert horseman and proved himself an able leader.

Refusing to move to a reservation, the Quahadi became fugitives, hunting bison and raiding settlements. But time has run out for Parker and his followers. In their struggle for survival, they formed an alliance with other Native American groups aimed at expelling white hunters from the Plains. But the alliance crumbled.

With Parker's surrender, and the bison nearly extinct, farmers and ranchers are free to expand settlements in the Texas Panhandle. Many Texans said yesterday they were grateful to the U.S. Army for putting a stop to Native American raids.

But some said the whole episode would one day be seen as a tragedy.

"BUFFALO SOLDIER" VICTIM OF PREJUDICE

THE first African American to graduate from the Military Academy at West Point has been dismissed from the U.S. Army, *writes our defense correspondent, July 1, 1882.*

He was accused of stealing, and behavior "unbecoming an officer" while stationed in Texas.

Henry O. Flipper, who was born enslaved, attended West Point during the Reconstruction era. He became the first African American to be an officer in the 10th Cavalry of African Americans who fought in the Indian Wars, and are said to have been nicknamed "Buffalo Soldiers" by Native American people.

Flipper was removed from his duties as quartermaster at Fort Davis, and was later accused of lying to cover up the theft of $2,000. A court-martial found him innocent of stealing, but he was still dismissed. Flipper strongly defended his innocence, claiming white soldiers plotted against him.

Many Buffalo Soldiers, right, have endured racial prejudice from within the U.S. Army. In spite of this, they have achieved an outstanding military record on the American frontier.

NEW CONSTITUTION TO PRESERVE THE TEXAS SPIRIT

A NEW constitution for Texas, the sixth since independence from Mexico, was adopted yesterday as the basic law of the state, *writes our politics editor, February 16, 1876.*

It moves away from a centralized, high spending state government, requires lower salaries for public officials, and limits the powers of both the governor and the state legislature. Its far-reaching articles make provision for low taxes and locally controlled, racially segregated schools.

People are most divided over changes affecting education. Although the constitution provides free public schools, critics say that this could prove to be too expensive.

Rural communities welcomed the new constitution, saying it was more in keeping with the Texas spirit of independence and self-reliance than the unpopular 1869 constitution, drawn up under pressure from Washington, D.C., during the Reconstruction era.

It begins with a bill of rights, declaring Texas to be a free and independent state, subject only to the U.S. Constitution, and that all free men have equal rights.

The state legislature, comprising a Senate and a House of Representatives, is to hold biennial, or every other year, sessions. Most senior public officials, including judges, are to be elected by popular vote.

The constitution also establishes the University of Texas, and confirms what is today Texas A&M University. Some predict that the constitution, which resembles a detailed code of laws, will need to be substantially amended as Texas society changes.

A MAGNIFICENT SYMBOL OF PRIDE

By our architecture correspondent
April 22, 1888

THE new state capitol building in Austin opened to the public yesterday. It is a magnificent symbol of Texas pride.

Modeled after the domed capitol in Washington, D.C.—but even taller!—this huge building contains 392 rooms, 924 windows, and 404 doors.

It took six years to build the structure, which replaced an older building that had been destroyed by fire. Visitors yesterday declared the new structure a marvel of the state.

The new capitol is the result of a design competition won by architect Elijah E. Myers. The crowning glory is the Goddess of Liberty statue atop its huge dome. The goddess holds a lowered sword in her right hand, while her left hand raises the Lone Star. Looking up 300 feet to the capitol's peak, her face can still be seen, as her features have been cleverly exaggerated.

The 1876 Constitution set aside 3 million acres of public land in the Texas Panhandle to fund the new capitol's construction.

A Chicago company was eventually assigned the contract to build it in exchange

ONE of America's earliest known serial killers, named the "Servant Girl Annihilator" by writer O. Henry, targeted Austin a few years before "Jack the Ripper" committed a string of London murders. In 1888, a newspaper claimed the Texas killer and Jack were the same man, causing British authorities to question U.S. cowboys. The Austin killings stopped after vigilante patrols began, but the murderer was never found.

for the land, valued at $1.5 million. They have used the land to organize the XIT Ranch, one of the largest cattle ranches in North America.

State leaders made clear they wanted Texas stone to be used for the building. Limestone near Austin contained iron particles that would produce rust stains, so pink-red granite rock from Granite Mountain in Burnet County was chosen, and a railroad was constructed to transport it.

Expert granite cutters came from Scotland for the job. But controversially, convict laborers were used to dig the stone.

The structure still needs to be completed, but that isn't stopping a week of celebrations next month. After many turbulent years of history, Texas is finally coming of age, and this building is the proof.

REVOLUTION IN FARMING

By our agriculture correspondent
December 31, 1887

FIRST it was barbed wire fencing, now it is the modern windmill that is transforming farming in Texas. The XIT Ranch, one of the largest in North America, has begun using windmills capable of pumping water from beneath the ground. They are sure to be used extensively by others too, including the giant King Ranch.

As windmills become a common sight in Texas, farms and ranches suffering from the state's dry climate are gaining access to life-giving water supplies. Vast new areas of land can now be farmed, making it possible for settlements to extend westward across Texas.

It is not only the new generation of windmills that is bringing about a revolution in Texas agriculture. The great cattle drives are dying out with the invention of barbed wire and railroad expansion.

Barbed wire fencing is ending the open range. Its recent popularity is due in large part to the skilled salesman John "Bet-a-million" Gates. He made news in San Antonio by erecting a fence to restrain longhorn cattle. He claims that his wire is "light as air, stronger than whiskey, and cheap as dirt." Sales have grown rapidly, making Gates his fortune.

Even Charles Goodnight, called the "father of the Texas Panhandle" by some, and a pioneer of the open range, has fenced along the Palo Duro Canyon, enclosing herds to control livestock breeding.

But the use of barbed wire has also provoked conflict. Herders have protested against fencing off water holes and grazing grasses, which they rely on for their cattle. A group of cattlemen called the "night nippers" resorted to cutting the wire, destroying millions of dollars of fencing. They stopped only after fence cutting was declared illegal.

The wire fences could spell the demise of longhorn cattle, which are more suited to the open range. Cattlemen say they will be sad to see these magnificent animals disappear.

DEATH OF THE LAWLESS "OLD WEST"

By our crime correspondent
August 20, 1895

TEXAS outlaw John Wesley Hardin was shot and killed in El Paso yesterday after a murderous career. His death is one more signal of the decline of the "Old West," where gunmen roamed the lawless U.S. frontier.

The son of a Methodist preacher, Hardin had more than 30 notches on his gun—evidence that he was the most dangerous gunman of all time in Texas, or so people say. For Hardin's part, he maintained that he only shot to save his own life, but he was known for exaggerating and making up stories.

Hardin's violent career started when he was just a boy. Aged 15, Hardin shot and killed an African American man in an argument after a chance meeting. With authorities looking for him, he fled to his brother's Texas home. He claimed to have killed three Union soldiers who sought to arrest him there.

Later, he rode up the Chisholm Trail, allegedly killing seven people along the way

and three more when he arrived in Abilene, Kansas. In Comanche, he killed a deputy sheriff named Charles Webb. From then on, he was on the run from law enforcement agents until he was captured.

Hardin was put on trial for Webb's murder and sentenced to 25 years in prison, where he made numerous but failed attempts to escape.

THE sport of "rodeo"—from the Spanish meaning "roundup"—grew out of the cattle industry as cowboys challenged each other in bronco riding and roping. Later, some showed their skills at "Wild West" events. One of the earliest rodeos on record was held in Pecos in 1883, which was the first to award prizes. The first indoor rodeo took place in Fort Worth.

While in jail, he also read many books about religion and studied law. He was pardoned last year and allowed to practice as a lawyer.

Hardin moved to El Paso to start a new life and a law practice, but it was not long before he was in trouble again. He hired several men to kill a rival, but yesterday one of the hired killers shot Hardin after a supposed argument. Hardin died instantly.

The frontier has a way to go before it is finally tamed. Despite the efforts of Texas Rangers to curb lawlessness, crime is everywhere. According to one correspondent who recently visited Texas: "There are said to reside not fewer than 20,000 ruffians who are 'wanted' in other states. . . . It is not agreeable to live under the rule of the revolver, especially for honest men of quiet disposition."

Justice of the Peace Roy Bean is making some progress from his base in Langtry, though his legal rulings can appear strange. Nicknamed the "Law West of the Pecos," he once fined a corpse $40 for carrying a concealed weapon, thus providing funeral expenses.

QUEEN CITY OF THE GULF LEFT IN RUINS

HURRICANE DESTROYS BUILDINGS AND CLAIMS THOUSANDS OF LIVES

By our weather correspondent
September 9, 1900

CITIZENS of Galveston today stared at the ruins of their once great port city in shock and horror. In less than a day, a deadly hurricane destroyed at least one third of the city's buildings and claimed the lives of more than 6,000 of its people.

The city is reeling from the worst natural disaster in U.S. history.

The scale of destruction is hard to understand: more than three-quarters of the population of 38,000 have been left homeless, according to one estimate.

The tragedy started to unfold late last month when a tropical storm was detected east of the Caribbean Sea. Moving steadily north, it began to strengthen. By the time it reached the Gulf of Mexico, it had grown into a hurricane. With wind speeds reaching 120 miles an hour or more, the hurricane made landfall on the Texas coast yesterday, and Galveston took the hardest hit.

Homes near the beach began falling first, as the storm lifted bricks, lumber, and roof tiles, launching the debris at other buildings. Later, a storm surge caused a sudden rise in water levels, flooding the city. The water's force knocked buildings off their foundations, pushing them ahead "like a battering ram." The victims included children and nuns at a Catholic orphanage.

One survivor described the horror: "My residence went down with about 50 persons who had sought it for safety, and all but 18 were hurled into eternity." It was about 10:00 p.m. when the tide finally began to fall.

The city's fate was not known for some time because bridges to the mainland and telegraph lines had been destroyed. The death toll runs into thousands, as only a few residents evacuated the city before the bridges fell. Many were drowned, others crushed by debris.

So numerous are the dead that the authorities plan to bury the bodies at sea or even burn them on beaches. Meanwhile, rescue workers are on the way from Houston to begin the desperate search for survivors. The American Red Cross will also help disaster victims.

JOPLIN IS RAGTIME KING

TEXAS composer and pianist Scott Joplin has been hailed the "King of Ragtime," after creating a musical sensation with his song "Maple Leaf Rag," *writes our culture editor, September 30, 1899.*

The sheet music, published in late summer, has taken America by storm and is on the way to selling thousands of copies. Music critics are already proclaiming it a classic to inspire generations.

Joplin, whose father had been enslaved, was born shortly after the Civil War and grew up in Texarkana. He played banjo at the age of seven and later enrolled in a segregated college to study piano and music theory. For a time, he was an entertainer at a club named the Maple Leaf.

The musician believes that education is the key to success for African American people.

A JAPANESE farmer has been credited with establishing the Gulf Coast rice industry. Seito Saibara came to Texas in 1903 after Houston business leaders invited him to teach rice production to local farmers. His Japanese colony at Webster began rice farming, the first crop grown from a gift of seeds from the Emperor of Japan. Other Asian groups have also settled in Texas, including Chinese—the first to arrive—Filipino, Korean, and Vietnamese people.

SPINDLETOP STARTS BLACK GOLD RUSH

By our industry correspondent
January 11, 1901

OIL! A gusher shot "black gold" 100 feet into the air yesterday after a major oil field was discovered in Texas. The find promises to transform the fortunes of the Lone Star State.

Located in a salt dome at Spindletop, near Beaumont, the discovery is the result of a drilling operation led by Anthony F. Lucas and marks the birth of the petroleum industry. Pipelines and refineries will be built in the state, many of them by newly created oil companies. All of this cheap fuel will revolutionize transportation and commerce in America.

Much of the credit for Spindletop goes to Pattillo Higgins. He was the first to explore the site for oil and gas, and later helped Lucas acquire a lease to drill on it.

Lucas made his momentous breakthrough yesterday after successfully drilling into the dome's sands. Mud began bubbling from the hole before six tons of drilling pipe came shooting up out of the ground. After several minutes of quiet, mud, then gas, then oil spurted out—and it is already flowing at the rate of 100,000 barrels of crude oil a day! Lucas' men are now battling to cap the gusher to bring it under control.

The news has captured the world's imagination. No one has ever seen such a gusher, and "wildcatters" and other oil speculators are stampeding to Texas in search of more oil fields. According to one report, so many people are rushing to Beaumont that it is difficult to find places to stay.

It's impossible to say how many barrels of oil Spindletop will produce, but experts predict it could run into millions. The discovery, however, is bad news for local farmers, already struggling with water shortages. Until the well is capped, they must watch with horror as their fields are flooded with oil.

Overnight, the "Gusher Age" has been born. Land prices around Spindletop are sure to increase wildly as buyers race to cash in. One man, who has been trying to sell land there for $150 for the past three years, is now expecting offers of $20,000 or more. In the search for new gushers, some wildcatters will make their fortunes, but many are just as likely to lose everything.

GERMAN PLOT THREATENS TEXAS

By our defense correspondent
March 4, 1917

TEXANS have pledged to fight to the death after a secret telegram revealed that Germany is trying to form an alliance with Mexico against the United States. Arthur Zimmermann, a high ranking German official, sent a coded note to German representatives in North America. The note proposes that in the event of America entering World War I, Germany would help Mexico regain the lands "stolen" by the United States, including Texas, Arizona, and New Mexico.

British intelligence intercepted and decoded the note in January, but it was only yesterday that Zimmermann publicly admitted the telegram was real. The revelation has outraged Americans, and conflict with the German Empire now seems even more likely. President Wilson is expected to ask the U.S. Congress to declare war against Germany within weeks.

According to diplomatic sources, Germany is hoping the Mexican government will declare war on America. It wants to divert U.S. military support away from the British and French Allies in Europe by tying down American troops on the Mexican border.

Texas, meanwhile, will not hesitate to put itself on a war path. Plans are being drawn up to mobilize thousands of young men to be soldiers, and hundreds of women are expected to serve in the Nurse Corps. The Lone Star State also has many military training bases, including airfields for recently invented airplanes.

SAN ANTONIO teacher Adina De Zavala fought to preserve the Alamo as a historical landmark. In the early 1900s, she barricaded herself inside its rat-infested barracks until authorities agreed to save them. Granddaughter of Lorenzo de Zavala, first Vice President of the Texas Republic, she campaigned for flying the Texas flag on March 2 to commemorate Texas Independence Day, the day in 1836 when Texas became a republic.

A GREAT DAY FOR DEMOCRACY

By our politics editor
June 29, 1919

TEXAS yesterday became the ninth state of the Union—and the first in the South—to approve the 19th Amendment to the U.S. Constitution, giving women the right to vote. The amendment allows women to vote in national and state elections, and makes it illegal to stop people from voting because of their gender.

The historic event follows years of campaigning by suffragists and is a triumph for organizations such as the Texas Equal Suffrage Association (TESA), led by Minnie Fisher Cunningham of Galveston, pictured right. Campaigners overcame stiff opposition, and hailed the victory as a great day for democracy—and a great day for women.

The amendment was submitted to U.S. states for approval earlier this month. The Texas legislature convened a special session on Monday. The next day, the House of Representatives approved the amendment, and the Senate approved it yesterday.

Cunningham, who moved to Austin two years ago, now plans to pursue governors "all over the West" to urge more states to approve the amendment.

One friend of the suffragist cause has been Governor William P. Hobby who last year signed a law to allow Texas women to vote in primary elections to choose political candidates.

For generations, many men—and even some women—have believed that if women were allowed to participate in politics and government, they risked neglecting their homes and children. Suffragists pointed out that women are citizens and should be allowed to have a voice in government affairs. Some white campaigners have been reluctant to recruit African American suffragists due to fears they might deter some supporters.

MEXICAN REVOLUTION BRINGS CHAOS AND BRUTALITY TO TEXAS

JACK JOHNSON, son of a former enslaved man, was the first African American to win the world heavyweight boxing championship. Born in Galveston, he became a professional prizefighter, which was illegal in Texas at the time. In 1910, he kept the world title by defeating Jim Jeffries, a white boxer who earlier had refused to cross the "color line" to fight him.

A TEJANO legislator is demanding an investigation into alleged brutality by Texas Rangers toward Hispanic people caught up in the Mexican Revolution, *writes our civil rights correspondent, February 1, 1918.*

José T. Canales is calling for reform following reports that the Rangers and others appointed by the state have killed thousands of Hispanic people on the Texas–Mexico border.

Mexicans have been fleeing across the border into Texas to escape a bloody revolution in their home country. But U.S. and state authorities fear that violence and disorder in Mexico may spill over into Texas. The situation took a turn for the worse in 1915, when some Mexican nationalists supported a manifesto called the "Plan of San Diego." The document called for the formation of a "Liberating Army of Races and Peoples" to "free" Texas and other southwestern states. Some say it was devised by a German spy.

The plan prompted raiders from Mexico to kill Anglos. As the Texas border descended into racial conflict, the Rangers retaliated by going on killing sprees.

Canales—who was born into a wealthy, land-owning family in Nueces County—now plans to bring the Rangers to account. Distrust between residents and Rangers runs deep, and it could take years for relations to improve.

Bonnie and Clyde slain in trap set by former Ranger

By our crime correspondent
May 24, 1934

TEXAS outlaws Bonnie Parker and Clyde Barrow were brought to justice yesterday, slain in a surprise attack on a lonely Louisiana road.

Thanks to brilliant detective work by former Texas Ranger Frank Hamer, the ruthless murderers were tracked down close to their hideout. At 9:15 a.m., the pair drove into Hamer's trap, where a posse was waiting. When the desperadoes ignored a command to halt, the officers gunned them down in a hail of bullets.

The couple's life of crime has enthralled Depression-era America. Bonnie, from Rowena, was working in a Dallas café before meeting Clyde, born near Telico. They soon began robbing grocery stores, gas stations, and small banks. On the run from the law, they gunned down officers who tried to arrest them.

The couple traveled throughout Texas, Oklahoma, Kansas, and other states, and settled for a time in Missouri with Clyde's brother. But neighbors began complaining to police about these rowdy residents. When officers arrived, they were met with a spray of bullets. Bonnie and Clyde escaped, leaving behind two dead lawmen and six rolls of film containing photographs of the couple, below.

Hamer was hired by the Texas prison service to track down the terrible twosome. He has helped to restore the Rangers' reputation and is expected to be honored by the U.S. Congress for outstanding crime-fighting.

BRAVE BESSIE

TRAGIC FATE OF FIRST FEMALE AFRICAN AMERICAN PILOT

By our aviation correspondent
May 1, 1926

TEXAS-BORN Bessie Coleman, America's first woman pilot of either African American or Native American descent, died yesterday in a flying accident. She was 34. Her daredevil stunts made her one of the greatest female fliers in the world.

Coleman was born in Atlanta, Texas, to an African American mother and a father of Native American and African American parentage.

She moved to Chicago as a young woman after dropping out of college when she ran out of money. She dreamed of flying airplanes and worked hard to save money for lessons. But flying schools refused to admit her because of her race.

Determined to reach her goal, Coleman then took language classes and traveled to France to qualify as a pilot. Her dream came true at a flying school near Paris, where she received one of the first known pilot's licenses issued to an African American.

"Brave Bessie" will be remembered for her stunt-flying and wing-walking—walking on the plane's wings in flight! Amazed crowds would flock to see her daredevil performances high overhead.

Coleman used her earnings from these shows to buy three Army surplus Curtiss biplanes and open her own flying school. But fate was not on her side. Yesterday, during a test flight in Jacksonville, Florida, her plane went into an uncontrolled dive. Coleman was not wearing a parachute and plunged to her death.

Her life story is an inspiration to people around the world and is sure to energize a new generation of African American and Native American people as well as women of all races. To her many fans, she will always be known as Bessie, the woman who "dared to dream."

A NATIONWIDE ban on the sale of alcoholic beverages divided Texas during the 1920s. Morris Sheppard, a U.S. Senator from Texas, was called the "father of national Prohibition" after championing the 18th Amendment to the U.S. Constitution. Federal agents tried to enforce the law across America, but organized crime gangs made fortunes from trading in illegal alcohol. Galveston became "sin city," a bustling center of illegal sales. Prohibition ended in 1933.

WASPS FLY INTO AVIATION HISTORY

WOMEN ARE TRAINED AS WARTIME PILOTS TO AID U.S. MILITARY CAMPAIGN

By our defense editor
August 6, 1943

THEY are called the WASPs of Texas. A new organization has been formed to train women to be pilots as part of the U.S. military campaign in World War II. The Women's Airforce Service Pilots—or WASPs—will help make up for the shortage of male pilots, most of whom are off fighting in the war.

The women are being trained at Avenger Field in Sweetwater, under the direction of famous aviator Jacqueline Cochran.

The WASPs will fly every type of American military aircraft, moving planes to new locations, delivering cargo and passengers, and testing aircraft all over the country.

Thousands of women are expected to apply but will need a pilot's license and will have to pay their way to get there, even though

men do not. They will not be considered on active military duty, though many of their tasks are vital to the U.S. war effort—and they will face many challenges and risks in their role.

It is a historical moment as women's responsibilities are often confined to the home and family, and the WASPs are overcoming doubts that women are capable of flying military planes.

Meanwhile, Texas can lay claim to being one of the largest military training grounds in World War II. As a major global oil power, the Lone Star State is also helping provide fuel for the U.S. war effort.

Japanese, German, and Italian residents of Latin American countries have been deported to the U.S., and many are being placed in Texas internment camps, or wartime detention centers, such as Seagoville and Crystal City. They are deemed a potential security threat to the

Allies, but many complain they are being sent to the U.S. as a result of racial prejudice.

Even before the U.S. entered the war, Texas Rangers showed their fighting spirit. The story goes that retired rangers—including

Frank Hamer, who tracked down crime duo Bonnie and Clyde— offered to help Britain's King George VI protect his country against the threat of a Nazi invasion. Their offer, however, was not taken up.

WAR HEROES HELP AMERICA TO VICTORY

TEXAS can take pride in its many war heroes who have helped America and its Allies defeat Nazi Germany, Italy, and Japan in World War II, *writes our war correspondent, September 3, 1945.*

Of the 750,000 Texans in the U.S. armed services, 33 have been awarded the Medal of Honor. Audie Murphy is one of the most decorated combat soldiers, receiving many awards and citations for bravery.

In France earlier this year, Murphy personally killed or wounded about 50 Germans and stopped an attack by enemy tanks. With his good looks, Murphy, pictured left, has become the pin-up boy of World War II.

Other Lone Star heroes include

Doris Miller, born near Waco, who is the first African American hero of World War II. He was assigned to USS *West Virginia* as a mess attendant. During the Japanese attack on Pearl Harbor, Miller fired at Japanese planes until forced to abandon ship. Awarded the Navy Cross, he later perished when his ship was torpedoed.

Two of America's victorious leaders are Chester W. Nimitz, a German Texan appointed Commander in Chief of the U.S. Pacific Fleet after Pearl Harbor, and Dwight D. Eisenhower, born in Denison, who served as Allied Supreme Commander in Europe.

Oveta Culp Hobby was the first director of the Women's Army Corps, while sailor Leonard Roy

Harmon died in action protecting a shipmate. Samuel Dealey, who was also killed in action, is another decorated naval hero.

Cleto L. Rodríguez is one of many Mexican Americans awarded the Medal of Honor for helping to defeat a Japanese force during the battle for Manila.

MEXICAN-AMERICAN labor organizer Emma "La Pasionara" Tenayuca led the Pecan Shellers Strike of 1938—one of the largest labor protests in Texas history. Some 12,000 women, mainly Mexican Americans, shelled over half the nation's pecans for very low pay. The workers won a pay raise, but machines later put many out of work.

KILBY INVENTION PROMISES EXCITING ERA OF TECHNOLOGY

By our science correspondent
September 13, 1958

DALLAS-BASED engineer Jack Kilby has invented an electronic part that promises to revolutionize the technology industry.

He demonstrated his "integrated circuit" to senior staff at Texas Instruments yesterday. The first circuit of its kind, experts say it paves the way for the computer "microchip." They predict it will unleash change similar to the Industrial Revolution by making the digital age possible. His invention is proof that Texas is branching out into new industries: first ranching and farming, then oil production, and now a pioneer in technology.

Kilby, pictured right, who recently joined Texas Instruments, must surely be a candidate for the Nobel Prize in Physics. He has created an interconnected circuit that is made from a single semiconductor material—in the case of Kilby's demonstration, a slice of the chemical element germanium.

Along with other engineers in America, he tackled a problem of circuit design called the "tyranny of numbers." Right now, to increase a computer's performance requires a huge number of extra components wired to each other by soldering, making the machine unreliable.

Not only does Kilby's "semiconductor chip" get rid of wires and faulty connections, it makes the entire circuit much more compact.

It is expensive to use germanium to make the circuit, so his invention will need to employ a cheaper alternative if it is to be made in large numbers.

Texas Instruments goes from strength to strength. The company's origins can be traced to two physicists who moved to Dallas in 1930. One of its successes was supplying components for the first portable transistor radio in 1954.

It may not be long before Texas Instruments builds the first hand-held calculator that uses the "brains" of a computer microchip.

34TH PRESIDENT OF THE U.S.
SON OF TEXAS IS ELECTED TO LEAD AMERICA

By our politics editor
November 4, 1952

IKE by a landslide! Gen. Dwight D. Eisenhower was elected the 34th President of the United States today. With his running mate, Richard M. Nixon, he won 39 states and a record popular vote of 34 million.

During the campaign, Eisenhower made dozens of speeches and traveled thousands of miles across America by air and rail. Known as "Ike" to millions, the Texas-born candidate also used short TV commercials to get his message across.

This is a day for Texans to be proud, as Ike was born in Denison, making him the first U.S. president whose birthplace is the Lone Star State. His father was employed by the Missouri-Kansas-Texas Railroad. And the modest home where he was born shows his working-class upbringing.

Ike served as Supreme Commander of the Allied Expeditionary Force in Europe in World War II and directed the D-Day invasion of Normandy. His reputation for staying calm under pressure makes him an excellent

MEXICAN Americans were excluded from serving on many juries across Texas. In 1954, the U.S. Supreme Court ruled this discrimination illegal in the case *Hernández v. the State of Texas*. It also decided that Mexican Americans and other nationality groups—as distinct from racial groups—must be treated equally under the law. The ruling was a triumph for Texas lawyer Gustavo C. García and Latino civil rights campaigners.

choice for president in the midst of the Cold War. National security is a top priority in the nuclear age.

In years to come, Denison citizens will want to erect a plaque to their "most distinguished son," and dedicate it to young people "that they may be inspired to greatness."

A tragic day for Texas, America, and the world

By our chief reporter
November 22, 1963

JOHN F. KENNEDY, 35th President of the United States, was shot to death earlier today by a hidden gunman. Kennedy, 46, lived for about an hour after a sniper cut him down as his open-top limousine left downtown Dallas.

Kennedy was rushed to Parkland Hospital, where frantic efforts were made to save his life. Sadly, the president did not survive.

The great office of president now falls to Vice President Lyndon B. Johnson, a native Texan, who had been riding two cars behind Kennedy's limousine. Johnson, mercifully, was not hit.

Texas governor John Connally and his wife had been riding in the same car as the president and Mrs. Kennedy. Connally was seriously wounded, but he is expected to recover.

According to reports, First Lady Jacqueline Kennedy cradled her dying husband's head in her lap as the presidential limousine sped to the hospital.

Before his death, Kennedy was administered the last rites of the Roman Catholic Church. Pictured right at Rice University in Houston, he was the first Catholic president in U.S. history.

There are conflicting accounts from eyewitnesses about the number of shots and the location of the gunman, but two shots probably came from a nearby building. The police have launched a huge manhunt to find the assassin.

Dallas citizens, like the entire nation, are overcome with horror and grief. People have shock and disbelief on their faces, struggling to find words to express their emotions.

NEW DAWN FOR CIVIL RIGHTS

By our civil rights correspondent
August 7, 1965

CIVIL RIGHTS in America took a giant step forward yesterday, thanks to legislation brought by President Lyndon B. Johnson.

Texas-born Johnson, known as "LBJ," has shown he is determined to make equal rights the law of the land for all Americans. His civil rights laws are targeting centuries of segregation, discrimination, and injustice.

Johnson signed the Voting Rights Act into law yesterday. Civil rights heroes Martin Luther King, Jr. and Rosa Parks, pictured right—who famously refused to give up her bus seat to a white woman—both attended a signing ceremony.

The act bans literacy tests and other obstacles to voter registration. LBJ told Congress: "It is wrong—deadly wrong—to deny any of your fellow Americans the right to vote."

The new law follows last year's Civil Rights Act, which made segregation—requiring African Americans and whites to use separate public spaces—illegal in

most places, from bus stations to restaurants. It also barred segregation in federal programs. "This bill is going to be enacted because justice and morality demand it," Johnson said.

When President Kennedy was tragically assassinated in 1963, then-Vice President Johnson was quickly sworn in as 36th President. A year later, he won a landslide election victory to continue his presidency.

Around this time, many African Americans and Hispanic Americans were protesting for equal rights, and marches were taking place in Texas and other states. In Washington, D.C., King made an inspirational speech about his dream in which all people are treated equal.

LBJ has transformed these calls for justice into law. It is said that no other U.S. president, aside from Abraham Lincoln, has done more to advance civil rights than Johnson. But the unpopular Vietnam War is casting a shadow over his presidency.

IN 1966, Texas Western College (now the University of Texas at El Paso) made sporting history when its basketball team won a national title. The team had an all-African American starting line-up, and defeated an all-white University of Kentucky starting line-up—a first in an NCAA title game. Later, their triumph was immortalized in the movie *Glory Road*.

"THAT'S ONE SMALL STEP FOR [A] MAN, ONE GIANT LEAP FOR MANKIND"

By our space correspondent
July 21, 1969

HOUSTON... The Eagle has landed. These are the first public words of NASA astronaut Neil Armstrong informing the world that Apollo 11's lunar module had landed safely on the Moon. It marks the birth of a new era in human history and exploration.

Armstrong yesterday became the first man to set foot on the Moon, stepping onto its dusty surface in the Sea of Tranquility. As he put his left foot down first, he declared: "That's one small step for [a] man, one giant leap for mankind." He described the surface as being fine-grained, like powder.

The historic event was captured on a television camera installed on the Eagle. It is said that one in every four people around the world watched some or all of the spell-binding images.

There are still potential dangers ahead. The Apollo 11 commander spent his first few minutes on the Moon taking photographs and soil samples in case the mission has to be aborted suddenly. Soon after, he was joined by colleague Edwin "Buzz" Aldrin, and the two collected data and performed various exercises—including jumping across the low-gravity landscape, which is said to feel like floating.

MILLIE Hughes-Fulford is one of more than 20 Texas-born astronauts. In 1991, she flew aboard Space Shuttle *Columbia* on the first Spacelab mission dedicated to life-science research. It was the first spaceflight to include three women. A fleet of reusable space shuttles sent more than 350 astronauts into space, but two missions ended in disaster, claiming 14 lives, including Amarillo-born Rick Husband.

Astronaut Michael Collins told Houston's Mission Control Center that he was successfully orbiting the Moon in the mother ship. The lunar module is expected to lift off later today to rejoin it in orbit.

Armstrong and Aldrin planted the U.S. flag on the Moon's surface and displayed a plaque with the inscription: "Here men from the planet Earth first set foot upon the Moon July 1969, A. D. We came in peace for all mankind."

This has followed years of preparation at NASA's Manned Spacecraft Center, which opened in Houston in 1963. A year earlier, President Kennedy set a goal of putting Americans on the Moon by the end of the decade. Led by inspirational managers such as Chris Kraft, Jr. and Gene Kranz, NASA's Mission Control Center is responsible for overseeing all U.S. human space flights.

Many sacrifices have been made along the way, including the deaths of Texas-born astronaut Ed White and two colleagues while training for the first Apollo mission.

By our politics editor
December 14, 2000

TEAM BUSH TAKES AMERICA
SON FOLLOWS FATHER TO THE WHITE HOUSE

TEXAS governor George W. Bush will follow in the footsteps of his father, George H. W. Bush, and become president of the United States.

He was elected the 43rd U.S. President in November, narrowly defeating Vice President Al Gore in one of the closest presidential elections in U.S. history. Gore won the popular vote, but Bush acquired more electoral college votes. Gore challenged the voting count in Florida, which had secured overall victory for Bush. The election result has now been confirmed in Bush's favor, making him the next president.

In a victory speech, Bush said: "Our nation must rise above a house divided . . . Together, guided by a spirit of common sense, common courtesy, and common goals, we can unite and inspire the American citizens."

Texans can boast of a father-and-son win, which has happened only once before in U.S. presidential history. Bush attended schools in Midland until the family moved to Houston. He has been Texas governor since 1995.

In his vision for America, he believes "compassionate conservatism" will find the common ground necessary to unite the nation. A key issue for the new president is education: he wants to ensure that every child in the U.S. will learn to read. He also wants to make healthcare affordable for everyone.

The new president's wife, Midland-born Laura Bush, was a teacher and librarian in Texas. She is expected to use her role as First Lady to promote literacy.

It is more than a decade since his father was elected 41st U.S. President. The Texas oil millionaire and World War II navy pilot is best remembered for his role in foreign affairs.

HOUSTON-BORN Barbara Jordan was elected to the U.S. House of Representatives from Texas in 1972, becoming the first African American woman from a southern state to serve in Congress. Earlier, she became the first African American state senator since the 1880s. She gained a national reputation for her role in the Watergate hearings.

He negotiated an agreement between the U.S., Canada, and Mexico to encourage trade between the three countries.

With the collapse of the Soviet Union, he helped reduce Cold War nuclear weapons and declared a partnership with Russia. He also authorized air and land attacks on Iraq after it invaded Kuwait but stopped the offensive before toppling its leader, Saddam Hussein.

His legacy has been preserved at the George H. W. Bush Presidential Library and Museum, which opened to the public on the campus of Texas A&M University in College Station.

LONE STAR STATE IS THRIVING CULTURAL HUB WITH AWARD-WINNING STARS

AUSTIN CITY LIMITS has been awarded the National Medal of Arts, the highest honor given to artists by the U.S. government, *writes our culture editor, November 13, 2003*.

The 29-year-old music program was presented with the prestigious award by President Bush yesterday. It is the only television show to be so honored.

The program was originally created to celebrate the music of Texas, but has gone on to showcase many musical styles performed by national and international stars, including Texas' own Stevie Ray Vaughan and George Jones.

The first show was broadcast in 1974 and starred Texas-born Willie Nelson, a country music legend.

Austin City Limits is one of the longest running music programs in U.S. television history. It remains as vibrant as ever, and has helped to build Austin's reputation as the "Live Music Capital of the World."

From Buddy Holly to Beyoncé, pictured right, Scott Joplin to Roy Orbison, Texas has made its mark on popular music. It has led the way in Tejano music with the likes of Lydia Mendoza and Selena, who was just 23 when she was killed.

The Lone Star State is a cultural hub, with world-class museums and orchestras. Houston is renowned for theater, and its ballet company for a time boasted Cuban sensation Carlos Acosta.

CENTURY OF SPORTS LEGENDS

DALLAS COWBOYS

SAN ANTONIO SPURS

By our sports editor
November 2, 2017

THE Houston Astros baseball team won the World Series yesterday—a first for the team and for Texas!

They beat the Los Angeles Dodgers four games to three to claim the title. The city plans to celebrate by cheering a victory parade that is certain to attract thousands.

The team's triumph crowns a century of Texas sporting excellence. The legendary Dallas Cowboys football team has won five Super Bowl championships, and has been known as "America's Team." The former Houston Oilers also won two league championships.

The San Antonio Spurs won their fifth NBA championship in 2014, recording one of the greatest winning streaks in modern basketball history. Other basketball champions have included the Dallas Mavericks and the Houston Rockets. The fabled Houston Comets won several WNBA championships.

In 1999, the Dallas Stars ice hockey team won the Stanley Cup.

Texas has excelled beyond team sports. Dallas-born Michael Johnson joined the ranks of the greatest track-and-field athletes after winning gold at the Sydney Olympics. He is the only male athlete to win both the 200- and 400-meter events at the same Olympic Games—in Atlanta.

In 1950, Babe Didrikson Zaharias was named "Woman Athlete of the Half Century." Texas-born, she became a role model for women after winning two gold medals in track-and-field at the 1932 Los Angeles Olympics. She later turned to golf, winning many Ladies Professional Golf Association championships.

In 1973, the Houston Astrodome was the venue for the so-called "battle of the sexes" tennis match when Billie Jean King beat Bobby Riggs.

The spirit of Texas burns bright in boxing. The "Galveston Giant" Jack Johnson was the first African American to win the world heavyweight boxing championship. Years later, Marshall-born Olympic gold medalist George Foreman claimed the world heavyweight crown.

One sports hero whose career was cut short was Freddie Steinmark, a Texas Longhorns football player, who died aged 22 in 1971. His fight against cancer inspired the U.S. "War on Cancer" and the making of a movie about his bravery.

Independence Day celebrates "Texas Mystique"

TODAY, on Texas Independence Day, the Lone Star State celebrates a unique heritage that has given rise to the "Texas Mystique," *writes our culture editor, March 2, 2019.*

This annual event marks the Texas Declaration of Independence on March 2, 1836, when Texas won its independence from Mexico and created the Republic of Texas.

Many Texans believe this spirit of self-reliance lives on, though Texas has changed beyond recognition. With about 29 million residents, the state is America's second most populous. The automobile is king in a landscape often dominated by skyscrapers and freeways. Houston and Dallas-Fort Worth are among America's largest urban areas.

Modern Texas is an economic powerhouse, one of the largest economies in the world. It remains a global center of the oil industry, while Houston is its energy capital. Texas is home to defense companies and has become a hub for technology and pioneering medical research. With more farms than any other state, agriculture remains important.

The state is multicultural and ethnically diverse. In the future, Latinos are expected to become its largest group.

The Texas legacy is a frontier mentality that values courage, strength, and independent-mindedness. Its citizens have tamed a vast, often inhospitable territory—and transformed it. But a growing issue is water resources.

Modern Texans are reaping the rewards of their heritage. The "Texas Mystique" is a shared belief that, somehow, they are special, different from other Americans. As the University of Texas at Austin says: "What starts here changes the world." So, what will be the Lone Star State's new frontiers?

A TIMELINE GUIDE TO
THE HISTORY OF TEXAS

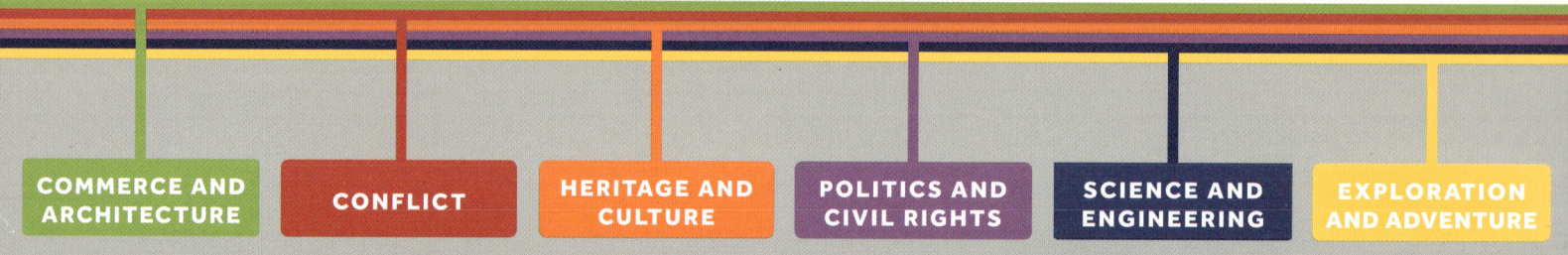

COMMERCE AND ARCHITECTURE **CONFLICT** **HERITAGE AND CULTURE** **POLITICS AND CIVIL RIGHTS** **SCIENCE AND ENGINEERING** **EXPLORATION AND ADVENTURE**

HOW TO USE THE TIMELINE

Unfold the pages and travel on an amazing journey to discover key events in the history of Texas, from earliest times to the present day. Each color represents a theme in the story. A selection of important moments in U.S. history helps show the bigger picture and highlights the influence that Texas has had on the nation and beyond.

On the back of the timeline, you will find a map of the Lone Star State and top places to visit, Texas flags, and a Texas Honor Roll. There is also a useful glossary to guide you through some of the concepts in *The Texas Chronicles*.

It all adds up to a remarkable story of people and events whose unique legacy can still be felt today in the 28th State of the Union.

TEXAS
FROM EARLIEST TIMES TO THE PRESENT DAY

225 million years ago
DINOSAURS roam a vast land that would become Texas, a state covering 268,000 square miles today. Twenty-one of the world's 300 known meat- and plant-eating types of dinosaur inhabit the region, until they become extinct. Later, mammoths, giant armadillo-like mammals, and other prehistoric animals dominate the land.

16,000 years ago
HUMANS migrate to Texas to hunt big game, such as mammoths and bison. One inhabitant is a 30-year-old woman, nicknamed "Midland Minnie." Found in Texas in 1953, her bones are some of the oldest discovered in the Americas, dating from about 10,000 years ago, or more.

1519
THE SPANISH are among pioneers in global exploration and claim lands in the Americas. One explorer, Alonso Álvarez de Pineda, and his men sail west from Florida along the Gulf Coast in search of a water route to Asia. They are credited as the first Europeans to see and map the coast of Texas.

500 years ago
TEXAS is home to many Native American groups besides Caddos. Jumanos hunt bison and trade. Gulf Coast Karankawas catch fish; Coahuiltecans eat a diet including pecans, armadillos, and snakes. For many, life changes when European people bring horses.

1534
ESTEVANICO is the first enslaved African person to travel across Texas. He joins Cabeza de Vaca and two others—the "Four Ragged Castaways"—who escape native peoples and walk about 2,400 miles to freedom. Later, Estevanico will be killed on an expedition toward lands visited by the castaways.

1629
THE FRANCISCANS arrive in Texas to try to convert native peoples to Christianity. The Jumanos say a "Lady in Blue" had already "visited" them with religious teachings. Meanwhile, a nun in Spain, known for her blue cloak, has visions of talking to native peoples. What actually happened? The mystery lives on to this day.

1685
FRENCH explorer René Robert Cavelier, Sieur de La Salle, accidentally lands on the Gulf Coast of Texas. La Salle establishes a colony, later named Fort St. Louis. The colony fails, and La Salle is killed by his own men. The Spanish search for these French "invaders," but find the colony has perished.

---

250 million years ago — **1 CE** — **1500s** — **1600s** — **170...**

4,500 years ago
ARTISTS create rock art pictures in canyons and natural shelters along the Pecos and Devils rivers, and Rio Grande. Using plant leaves as brushes, they paint murals of spear throwers, deer, panthers, and healers called "shamans." The art's meaning remains a mystery, but suggests complex cultures.

1,500 years ago
HAVING arrived in Texas as hunter-gatherers, Native American people called the Caddo begin to farm corn and other crops. They create beautiful pottery, which they trade far and wide. One ancient trail leads to the "Caddo Mounds" complex, where mounds made of earth are used for ceremonies.

1528
SPANISH conquistador Álvar Núñez Cabeza de Vaca is washed ashore with other men near Galveston Island. They are the first Europeans to set foot on Texas soil. Many die of sickness and hunger. Cabeza de Vaca survives to publish his incredible story and will be called "the first historian of Texas."

1 PTA / IV CENTENARIO DE / CABEZA DE VACA

NEW SPAIN
LONG before Texas becomes part of the U.S., it is Spanish territory. New Spain is established after conquistador Hernán Cortés overthrows the Aztec Empire in 1521. The territory includes land that is known today as Mexico, Central America, much of southwestern and central United States—including Texas—and Florida. Silver is discovered in Zacatecas in the 1540s, and mining becomes a major activity in New Spain.

1598
EL PASO lays claim to one of the earliest Thanksgivings in North America. Explorer Juan de Oñate celebrates his expedition's survival of an arduous march to the Rio Grande. De Oñate claims all lands draining into the river as Spanish territory. Spanish influence over Texas and the southwest slowly begins.

17...
SA... / the... / Va... / the... / El... / "r... / An... / cla... / Th... / fo...

1690
TO PROTECT their em... against the French, th... Spanish begin buildin... fortified missions in T... which are guarded b... presidios. Franciscan... missions, seeking to... to Christianity native... who help build them. ... missions also run the... cattle ranches.

KEY

  PRE-U.S. AND U.S. HISTORY MOMENTS

See back of Timeline for useful Glossary and Texas Honor Roll

William B. Travis (1809–1836)

Texas commander at the Alamo, whose "Victory or Death" plea for help has made the history books.

John Neely Bryan (1810–1877)

Explorer, trader, and pioneer who founded the town of Dallas in November 1841.

John O. Meusebach (1812–1897)

Played a key role in establishing German Texas and negotiated a lasting peace treaty with the Comanches.

Francita Alavez (dates not known)

The "Angel of Goliad," said to have saved many Texians by hiding them away before the Goliad Massacre.

John Coffee "Jack" Hays (1817–1883)

Texas Ranger and U.S.-Mexican War fighter, whose gun-toting men became the stuff of Ranger legend.

Mary Maverick (1818–1898)

Author of memoirs about life in early Anglo Texas, wife of Samuel Maverick—source for the word "maverick."

Homer Garrison, Jr. (1901–1968)

Texas Ranger chief, who turned his state law enforcement agency into world-class crime and corruption unit.

Juanita Craft (1902–1985)

Dallas civil rights activist, who devoted 50 years to National Association for the Advancement of Colored People.

Howard Hughes, Jr. (1905–1976)

Texas-born business tycoon, movie director, and record-breaking pilot, who founded a medical research institute.

Oveta Culp Hobby (1905–1995)

First director of the Women's Army Corps in World War II, who also served in the Eisenhower administration.

Lyndon B. Johnson (1908–1973)

36th U.S. President, who improved civil rights, healthcare, and education, despite Vietnam War setbacks.

Michael DeBakey (1908–2008)

Surgeon and medical scientist of Lebanese parents, who pioneered heart surgery and mobile army hospitals.

Kay Bailey Hutchison (1943–)

Galveston-born, the first woman to represent Texas in the U.S. Senate, and U.S. ambassador to NATO.

George W. Bush (1946–)

Texas governor and 43rd U.S. President, who declared a "war on terror" after the 2001 terrorist attacks.

Laura Bush (1946–)

Midland-born First Lady (wife of George W. Bush), who campaigns on education and women's health issues.

Jeana Yeager (1952–)

Aviator who co-piloted first global, non-stop, non-refueled flight and received a presidential medal.

Dr. Bernard Harris, Jr. (1956–)

Temple-born NASA astronaut who, during a space shuttle flight, is first African American to walk in space.

Michael Dell (1965–)

Houston-born businessman and philanthropist, who has created a global technology company.

Military dictatorship Political power centralized in one person's hands or in a small group, supported by the military

Missions Spanish frontier settlements run by Franciscans that saught to convert Native Americans to Christianity

Mustangs Wild horses

Paleontologists Scientists who search for and study fossils

Presidio A Spanish military garrison

Primary elections Elections in which candidates from one political party compete for a chance to run in the main election

Reconstruction Period after the Civil War when the U.S. government controlled the defeated Confederate states and ended slavery

Rough Riders Nickname for the 1st U.S. Volunteer Cavalry, led by Theodore Roosevelt in the Spanish-American War

Segregation Separation of people due to their race or nationality

Sharecroppers Farmers who give a portion of their crops as rent to landowners

Squatters Unlawful occupiers of a building or land

State A political entity of the U.S., with each state bound in a union with each other. Texas is the 28th state of the Union

State capital The seat of government of the state

State capitol The main state government building, not to be confused with the state capital

Suffragists Campaigners for women's right to vote

Tejanos Early Texas settlers of Hispanic descent; sometimes used today to refer to Mexican Texans

Texans Natives or inhabitants of the state of Texas

Texians Citizens of the Republic of Texas, or Anglo residents of Texas under Mexican rule

U.S. Supreme Court Interprets the law, and rules on whether individual actions of citizens or government officials are allowed under the U.S. Constitution

Vaqueros Early Spanish cowboys, from the Spanish word "vaca," meaning "cow"

Watergate A political scandal leading to the resignation of U.S. President Richard Nixon

Wildcatters Oil prospectors who sink exploratory wells

Lorenzo de Zavala (1788–1836)

Mexican-born Vice President of Texas, who helped draft Mexico and Republic of Texas constitutions.

Stephen F. Austin (1793–1836)

Founder of Anglo Texas, who established the first colony of Anglo settlers in Mexican-controlled Texas.

Sam Houston (1793–1863)

President of Texas and governor of Texas and Tennessee, defeated Mexico's Santa Anna in the Texas Revolution.

José Antonio Navarro (1795–1871)

Statesman and leader in the Texas Revolution, one of the 59 signers of the Texas Declaration of Independence.

Anson Jones (1798–1858)

Last president of the Republic of Texas, named the "architect of annexation" of Texas by the United States.

Mirabeau Buonaparte Lamar (1798–1859)

President of the Republic of Texas, who named Austin the capital and approved Lone Star Flag.

Jesse H. Jones (1874–1956)

Businessman and New Deal official, who, with his wife Mary, founded the philanthropic Houston Endowment.

Sam Rayburn (1882–1961)

Politician who holds the record as longest-serving Speaker of the U.S. House of Representatives.

Minnie Fisher Cunningham (1882–1964)

Suffragist and politician, who successfully campaigned for women to be given the vote in Texas and the U.S.

Chester W. Nimitz (1885–1966)

German Texan appointed Commander in Chief of the U.S. Pacific Fleet after Pearl Harbor in World War II.

Dwight D. Eisenhower (1890–1969)

Born in Denison, the the Allied Supreme Commander in Europe in World War II and 34th U.S. President.

Marcelino Serna (1896–1992)

Texas soldier hero in World War I and first Hispanic person to receive the Distinguished Service Cross.

Irma Lerma Rangel (1931–2003)

The first Mexican-American female legislator in Texas, who improved higher education in poor areas.

Larry Hagman (1931–2012)

Fort Worth-born actor, who gained a global audience for his portrayal of J. R. Ewing in TV show *Dallas*.

Ann Richards (1933–2006)

Second female governor of Texas, who helped revitalize the state's economy and led Texas prison reform.

Willie Nelson (1933–)

Abbott-born singer-songwriter and campaigner, renowned for his unique style of country music.

Eugene "Gene" F. Kranz (1933–)

NASA flight director best known for leading the first Moon landing and the Apollo 13 rescue teams.

Barbara Jordan (1936–1996)

The first African-American woman from a southern state to serve in the U.S. Congress.

GLOSSARY

Here are definitions for concepts found in *The Texas Chronicles*, including words marked in red on the timeline.

Adelsverein A society for German immigrants in Texas

Anglos White colonists during and after Mexican Texas

Annexation Takeover of a territory by a country, state, or city

Antebellum The period before a war, particularly the U.S. Civil War

Biennial Taking place every other year

Bronco A wild or half-tamed horse

Colony A group of settlers living together in a foreign place

Confederate States of America/ Confederacy A short-lived country formed by southern states splitting from the Union

Conquistadors Spanish military explorers

Constitution Basic principles of law governing a nation or state

Electoral college A group of representatives, each sworn to support a particular candidate, who represent the U.S. people in presidential elections

Emancipation The freeing of enslaved or disadvantaged people

Empresarios Spanish for "entrepreneurs," these settlers were granted land in return for recruiting other people to move to a colony

Federal A national government system that unifies states but also allows them to govern independently

Franciscans Members of religious orders within the Catholic Church founded by St. Francis of Assisi

Impeachment A charge of misconduct against a public official

Indian Territory Lands that the U.S. forced Native Americans to move to

Ku Klux Klan (KKK) A group of supremacists who believe whites are a superior race and target African Americans, Catholics, and Jews

Manifest Destiny A 19th-century belief that U.S. expansion from the Atlantic to the Pacific was certain to happen—and desirable

Maverick Independent-minded person, originating from Samuel Maverick who became known for not branding his cattle

Mexican Revolution This 20th-century conflict started as a protest against unjust government but became a civil war

1779

HAVING aided American Patriots, Bernardo de Gálvez, the Governor of Louisiana—then under Spanish control—helps defeat the British along the Gulf Coast during the Revolutionary War. He brings in Texas cattle to feed his troops. De Gálvez is made Viceroy of New Spain, and the coastal city of Galveston is later named for him.

1734

MOVING south in search of bison and **mustangs**, nomadic expert horsemen, called Comanches, are recorded near San Antonio. Through warfare and trade, their "Comanchería" empire will dominate the Southern Plains. Later, they clash with Anglo Americans laying claim to Texas.

1793

MISSION San Antonio de Valero closes. Like other missions in Texas, it had limited success in converting native peoples to Christianity. Later, troops from New Spain's Álamo de Parras occupy its quarters. It is forever after known as the Alamo. In 1805, it houses Texas' first hospital.

AMERICAN REVOLUTION

Thirteen American colonies declare independence from Great Britain in 1776. They are angry about paying British taxes without elected members representing them in the British parliament. With French and Spanish help, they defeat Britain in the Revolutionary War. The United States of America is born. A new **constitution** creates a **federal** system of national government.

1821

MANY Karankawas are killed in a failed attack to rescue one of the group's women, held by French pirate Jean Laffite's men on Galveston Island. The Karankawas, one of the native groups in Texas, later die out—victims of European diseases and conflict with Anglo and Tejano settlers.

1829

MEXICAN President Vicente Ramón Guerrero will become a national hero after abolishing slavery in Mexico. Despite the evils of slavery, Stephen F. Austin warns that Texas cannot create rich plantations without it. Guerrero avoids conflict by exempting Mexican-controlled Texas from general **emancipation**.

1830

ANGLOS leave the U.S. to escape debt, posting "Gone to Texas" on their abandoned homes. Mexico fears they will dominate the territory and rebel. It stops immigration, bans imports of enslaved people, and later imprisons Stephen F. Austin who calls for a breakaway Texas government.

1835

A SMALL cannon sparks the first conflict of the Texas Revolution. Challenging the **military dictatorship** of Mexico's Antonio López de Santa Anna, Gonzales settlers stop his troops reclaiming a town cannon. They are said to create a banner showing the cannon and the words "Come And Take It."

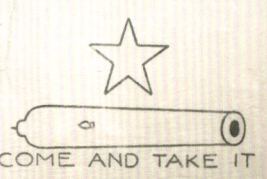

COME AND TAKE IT

0s — **1800s** — **1810s** — **1820s** — **1830s**

'18

N ANTONIO is founded with Mission San Antonio de ...ero and Bexar presidio. As Spanish presence grows, ...amino Real de los Tejas, or ...al road," will connect San ...onio and Nacogdoches, ...med to be Texas' oldest town. ...road is a vital supply line ...the missions and presidios.

LOUISIANA

NAMED for King Louis XIV, Louisiana is controlled by France for many of its early years. It borders the Texas territory claimed by New Spain, creating tensions with France. Under the Louisiana Purchase of 1803, France sells Louisiana and other lands to the U.S., and New Spain gets an ambitious new neighbor—the U.S.

1821

MEXICO invites settlers to Texas to develop the sparsely populated territory. **Empresario** Stephen F. Austin founds the first colony of **Anglos**—297 families or partnerships, nicknamed the "Old 300." Many bring enslaved people of African descent who make up about a quarter of the colony.

1835

LEGENDARY frontiersma... "Davy" Crockett leaves ... Tennessee home for Texa... had failed to get re-elect... U.S. Congressman after o... the enforced removal of N... Americans to west of the... Mississippi River. Before h... he tells voters that "They ... to hell, and I would go to ...

1758

A SPANISH mission, named Santa Cruz de San Sabá, is destroyed by Comanche, Wichita, and other Native American warriors. The mission was built for the Apaches in the territory of their mortal enemies, the Comanches. The Spanish try to restore their control but are forced to retreat.

1810

MEXICANS revolt against Spanish authority. Many **Tejanos** rally in support. Helped by Anglo volunteers, they declare independence. But they are defeated at Medina in 1813—the bloodiest battle in Texas history. Mexico breaks free from Spain and wins independence in 1821. Mexican rule over Texas begins.

1823

THE LEGEND of the Texas Rangers law enforcement agency is born. To protect his new colony, Stephen F. Austin funds ten men as "rangers for the common defense" to act against raids by native peoples who feel under threat. For their work, these citizen soldiers are offered payment in the "currency" of land.

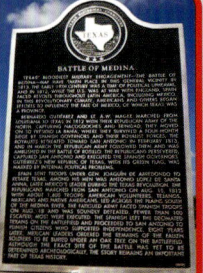

1836

A TEXAS force of 189 men bravely defends the Alamo fo... 13 days against a large Mexic... army. The defenders, includin... commander William B. Travis, James Bowie, and David Crockett, are killed, their bodie... burned. Travis' "Victory or Deat... letter goes down in history, an... the defenders' bravery is commemorated to this day.

1836
SAM HOUSTON defeats Santa Anna at the Battle of San Jacinto. His troops declare, "Remember the Alamo! Remember Goliad!" Some 900 Texians perform a near miracle in a battle of less than 20 minutes. Santa Anna is taken prisoner as 1,360 Mexican soldiers are killed or captured.

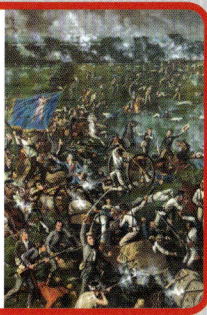

1839
THE LONE STAR flag is adopted by the Texas Congress and President Lamar. Red, white, and blue with one white star, it is the bold national symbol of the Republic of Texas and replaces the National Standard of Texas—a yellow star on a blue background. Later, it will become the flag of the "Lone Star State."

1845
TEXAS enters the Union as the 28th **State** after voters approve annexation of the republic by the U.S. A new constitution, modeled on those of other southern states, gives all white males the vote and upholds slavery. A ceremony will celebrate the historic moment, and Austin will become the official **state capital**.

1848
WORK starts on the construction of front under the direction Army's William J. W troops explore and e trails, the forts are us protect Texas settler pacify Native Americ parties. Worth dies year later, and Fort V named for him.

1836
THE TEXAS Declaration of Independence is signed in Washington-on-the-Brazos, proclaiming a "free, sovereign and independent republic." A constitution is modeled on the U.S. Constitution, and upholds slavery. Tejanos are among 59 who sign the declaration. Sam Houston is named chief of the army.

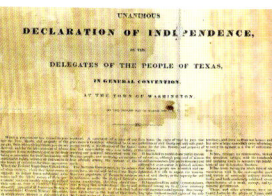

1836
COMANCHES attack Fort Parker and take hostages, including a young girl named Cynthia Ann Parker, below. For 25 years, she lives with the Comanches and marries Chief Peta Nocona. Her son Quanah Parker becomes a great Comanche leader. Texas Rangers later find her, but she struggles to adapt to Anglo society.

1839
PRESIDENT Lamar starts the Cherokee War, his latest attack on native peoples. After losing the Battle of the Neches, the Cherokees are forced to leave for U.S. **Indian Territory**. The Cherokee chief, Bowl, below, falls in battle and is shot by Texians who seize his sword, a gift given to him by "friend of the Cherokees" Sam Houston.

1844
GERMAN Prince Carl of Solms-Braunfels leads a Texas group, called the **Adelsverein**, to establish a German colony in the republic. As part of a plan to create a "New Germany," the Prince founds New Braunfels in 1845. Other German settlements follow, including Fredericksburg. Czech people also move to Texas.

1840s

avid

He
as
sing
ve

eaves,
ht go
as."

1836
THE REPUBLIC of Texas begins. The Treaties of Velasco end the war with Mexico, but it refuses to recognize Texas independence. Veterans of the Texas Revolution are rewarded with land. Voters elect Sam Houston—"Old Sam Jacinto"—as the republic's president. Many also support **annexation** by the U.S.

1842
MANY Tejanos are forced out by Anglos who pour into Texas after it wins its independence from Mexico. Tejano Senator Juan Seguín—a leader of the Texas Revolution who has a Texas city named in his honor—clashes with Anglo **squatters**. Mexico invades Texas again, and he falls under suspicion. He is forced to flee.

1847
GERMAN John O. Meuse strikes a deal with the Comanches living near G settlers. The Meusebach Comanche Treaty gives b groups the right to travel each other's territories an the native people gifts in for peace. It is one of the unbroken agreements be settlers and native people

1836

TEXIANS panic after the Alamo defeat and flee their homes. Texan commander James W. Fannin and his men confront Mexican forces, but surrender and are marched back to their Goliad fort as prisoners. Santa Anna, below, orders the execution of at least 340 of them. The news enrages Sam Houston's men.

1837
THE REPUBLIC of Texas operates its capital in the new city of Houston, named for Sam Houston, hero of San Jacinto. Under the republic's next president, Mirabeau B. Lamar, right, the capital moves to the hamlet of Waterloo. It is renamed Austin in honor of Anglo colonist Stephen F. Austin.

1843
INNKEEPER Angelina Eberly saves Austin as Texas capital in the "Archives War." She fires the town cannon to warn residents that men are taking government documents. They are acting on orders from Sam Houston, re-elected Texas president, who tries to move the capital back to Houston, away from the frontier.

1846
THE U.S. takeover of Texas provokes war with Mexico. The U.S. wins, and the 1848 Treaty of Guadalupe Hidalgo fixes the border at the Rio Grande. The U.S. gains Mexico's vast northern territories including California, the climax of its **Manifest Destiny**. Mexico recognizes Texas as part of the U.S.

TEXAS HONOR ROLL

Alonso Álvarez de Pineda (?–1520)

Spanish explorer, led the European expedition that first saw and mapped the coast of Texas.

Álvar Núñez Cabeza de Vaca (c.1490–c.1559)

Spanish explorer and first European to set foot on Texas land, who was washed ashore from a raft.

Estevanico (?–1539)

The first African enslaved person to cross Texas, he was later killed on an expedition.

Sieur de La Salle (1643–1687)

Explorer René Robert Cavelier, who founded a doomed French colony—later known as Fort St. Louis—in Texas.

David "Davy" Crockett (1786–1836)

Frontiersman, politician, Texas Revolution leader, and American folk legend, who died at the Alamo.

Henri Castro (1786–1865)

French-born, Jewish empresario, who recruited many French and German families to settle in Texas.

Milton M. Holland (1844–1910)

Formerly enslaved, the first African American Texan to earn the Medal of Honor in the Civil War.

Quanah Parker (c.1845–1911)

Comanche leader, son of Cynthia Ann Parker, became an influential spokesman for Native Americans.

Anthony Francis Lucas (1855–1921)

Croatian-born engineer, who discovered the Spindletop "gusher" to create the Texas oil boom.

Seito Saibara (1861–1939)

Farmer who founded a Japanese colony in Texas and is credited with creating the Gulf Coast rice industry.

John Nance Garner (1868–1967)

Texas native and Vice President to Franklin D. Roosevelt, who played a key role in the New Deal.

Annie Webb Blanton (1870–1945)

Suffragist and first woman elected to a statewide office, as superintendent of public instruction.

"Lady Bird" Johnson (1912–2007)

First Lady (wife of LBJ), who promoted environmental improvements to cities, including Austin.

Hector P. García (1914–1996)

Mexican-American physician, founder of the American G.I. Forum, a national voice for Mexican Americans.

Lydia Mendoza (1916–2007)

Acclaimed singer and guitarist of Tejano music, known as the "Lark of the Border."

Patricia Highsmith (1921–1995)

Internationally successful author, born in Fort Worth, famed for her Tom Ripley thrillers and others.

George H. W. Bush (1924–2018)

World War II veteran, Texas oil man, and 41st U.S. President, engaged U.S. forces in Iraq.

Christopher C. Kraft, Jr. (1924–)

NASA's first flight director, who founded Houston's Mission Control Center, now named for him.

Texas has three branches of state government, as well as local government.

EXECUTIVE
The executive branch implements and enforces laws and is led by the Governor who is also commander-in-chief of Texas military forces. Elected for a four-year term, the Governor has the power to approve or reject laws passed by the legislature.

LEGISLATIVE
The Texas legislature makes state laws. They are seated in the state capitol in Austin and hold a series of meetings every two years. The legislature is made up of 150 members of the Texas House of Representatives, each elected to two-year terms, and 31 members of the Texas Senate, whose terms last for four years.

JUDICIAL
The judiciary is composed of elected members of the Texas Supreme Court and the Texas Court of Criminal Appeals. It also includes lower courts that handle many civil and criminal cases. The Texas Supreme Court rules on constitutional matters affecting the state.

LOCAL GOVERNMENT
There are 254 counties in Texas, each one run by a Commissioner's Court—the largest number of any state. Cities can opt for "home rule" status, while special districts, such as Independent School Districts, also enjoy a large amount of independence.

U.S. GOVERNMENT
The power of the federal national government—originally created for collective defense of the states and foreign diplomacy—lies with the president of the United States, the U.S. Congress, and the U.S. Supreme Court in a system of "checks and balances." The Congress is made up of 435 elected members of the U.S. House of Representatives—36 from Texas—and 100 elected members of the U.S. Senate, two from each of the 50 states.

1853
TEXAS gets its first railroad—a segment of an 80-mile line between Harrisburg and Alleyton—built by the Buffalo Bayou, Brazos and Colorado Railway Company. Rail travel will change Texas forever. The state will one day have one of the longest railroad networks. Dallas will boom as a major center of railroad activity.

1865
OF 70,000 Texans fighting for the Confederacy, the Texas Brigade led by John Bell Hood, right, gains one of the finest reputations. It serves under Robert E. Lee who declares: "Texans always move them!" It surrenders after Lee's defeat at Appomattox. Later, the last land battle takes place on Texas soil—at Palmito Ranch.

1870
IN THE Reconstruction era, Matthew Gaines, a former enslaved man, serves as senator in the Texas legislature. He campaigns for the rights of freed African Americans, to improve education, and protect farm workers. Another African American, George T. Ruby, also serves in the Texas Senate.

187
TEXA
cons
inde
and t
limits
spen
bien
legis
Univ
confi
A&M

1861
THE CIVIL WAR breaks out. Texas splits from the Union, which opposes slavery, and joins the Confederate States of America, which support slavery. Texas governor Sam Houston, himself a slave owner, calls for the Union to stay together. He refuses to swear loyalty to the Confederacy and is removed from office.

1866
ONE of the greatest livestock migrations ever known begins. Cowboys herd millions of cattle out of Texas to feed the North in the years after the Civil War. The cowboys travel far and wide along a network of trails, including the Chisholm Trail, named for trader Jesse Chisholm of Scottish and Cherokee descent.

1870
TEXAS is one of the last states to be readmitted into the Union, after it finally approves the 13th, 14th, and 15th Amendments to the U.S. Constitution. The amendments abolish slavery, provide citizens with equal protection under the law, and give men the vote, whatever their "race, color, or previous condition of servitude."

1849
THE TEXAS prison system begins when its first occupant—a convicted horse thief—enters the Huntsville state prison. Later, prisoners across Texas will be hired out to work for railroads, mining companies, and plantations, and will help construct the state capitol building in Austin.

1875
WHITE hun
bison. This e
tragedy thre
supply and
peoples. In
Comanche
Parker and
groups are
people are
Territory res

1850s

1860s

1870s

1850
THE COMPROMISE of 1850 defines the northwestern borders of Texas, giving up its claim to New Mexico. Texas keeps the Panhandle—the part of the state that is farthest north—and the U.S. government takes over a public debt. The compromise means that slavery cannot automatically be extended into New Mexico.

1859
TEXAS grows to be a major "cotton state." With the forced removal of native peoples to Indian reservations, more land becomes available for growing crops. Anglo colonists continue to keep enslaved people to farm the land. Antebellum Texas has 182,000 enslaved people—nearly a third of its population.

1865
ON JUNE 19, Union General Gordon Granger declares in Galveston an end to slavery for 250,000 African Americans in Texas. It is two years after President Abraham Lincoln's Emancipation Proclamation. Forever a day of celebration, the event will become known as "Juneteenth."

1870
THE CHINESE are the first Asians to settle in Texas. Ma
work on the railroads and se
around El Paso. The Asian
population grows with the ar
of Japanese rice farmers an
Mexican-Chinese people in t
early 1900s. Other Asian gro
follow, including Filipino, Kor
and Vietnamese people.

AMERICAN CIVIL WAR
THE bloodiest war in U.S. history starts in 1861. Eleven southern states—the Confederacy—break from the Union. They fear that President Abraham Lincoln will end slavery, harming their farming economy that is built on enslaved labor. Lincoln issues the Emancipation Proclamation in 1863. The war ends in 1865 with the Union restored and slavery ended, but Lincoln is assassinated, and the southern states are devastated by war.

1867
U.S. ARMY units of African Americans serve in Texas on the frontier, escorting wagon trains, and often fighting in conflicts against Native American groups. The "Buffalo Soldiers"—said to be named by native people—overcome racial prejudice from white soldiers and settlers to achieve an outstanding record.

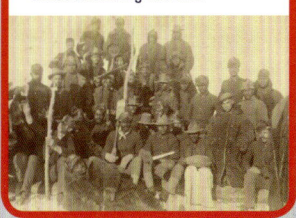

1872
SHARECROPPE
land to grow c
crops, giving a
landowner. Th
include freed
people as well
enter Texas fro
states devasta
also from Euro
any cash left o
live in debt an

1853
RIVERBOAT captain and businessman Richard King purchases land grants to build the King Ranch. He raises cattle, horses, and sheep, and, later, is one of the first to erect fences on open lands. The ranch grows to 614,000 acres by the time of his death, and is today bigger than the state of Rhode Island!

FLAGS OF TEXAS

The slogan "Six Flags Over Texas" describes the six powers that once controlled part or all of Texas: Spain, France, Mexico, the Republic of Texas, the Confederate States of America, and the United States of America. Their coats of arms can be seen beneath the state capitol dome in Austin. But the "Six Flags" are only part of the story. More than a dozen flags have left a mark on Texas history:

1. SPANISH FLAG

When Christopher Columbus set foot in the Americas in 1492, he was working for the Spanish government. Of all the European powers, Spain gained the largest empire in the Americas. The Spanish first set eyes on Texas in 1519 and greatly influenced its history and culture for the next 300 years. Spain was represented for a time by the flag of Castile and León, two Spanish kingdoms.

2. FRENCH FLAG

French explorer René Robert Cavalier, Sieur de La Salle, established a colony in 1685 that came to be known as Fort St. Louis. The colony collapsed after many perished from disease, and La Salle was killed in an ambush. Had it survived, France and Spain would almost certainly have clashed for influence over Texas.

3. MEXICAN FLAG

In 1810, the people of Mexico rebelled against Spanish rule, and after a decade of war, gained their independence. Texas formed part of Mexico at the time. The flag was adopted in 1821, bearing the colors of the revolutionary Mexican forces and the famous eagle-and-snake.

4. GONZALES FLAG

The first shots of the Texas Revolution took place in Gonzales, when Texians refused to return a cannon to the Mexican government. After the fight, the Texians are said to have designed a flag of a cannon, with the words "Come And Take It." This became a symbol of Texas independence.

5. 1824 TRICOLOR

In the early days of the Texas Revolution, some rebels wanted the federalist Mexican Constitution of 1824 restored. The eagle-and-snake of Mexico's tricolor (three-colored) flag were replaced with the number "1824." It is one of the earliest revolutionary flags.

6. TWO-STAR TRICOLOR

Although many Texians favored independence, some wanted to remain part of Mexico but have separate states for Texas and Coahuila, which had been joined together. A new version of the Mexican tricolor—supposedly flown at the Battle of the Alamo—displayed two stars to represent both states.

7. LONE STAR AND STRIPES

Alamo defenders may have flown this flag, too, as a popular symbol of the Texas Revolution. The single star represents the wish for Texas to be an independent country. Sam Houston's army also waved the flag at the Battle of San Jacinto, and it flew over Goliad as well. It later became the official flag of the Texas Navy.

8. NATIONAL STANDARD OF TEXAS

In September 1836, leaders of the Republic of Texas decided that the new nation deserved a new flag. Politician David Burnet proposed a design with a blue background and a single yellow star. It was adopted, but was never widely used.

9. LONE STAR FLAG

The second president of the Republic of Texas, Mirabeau B. Lamar, approved a new national flag for Texas in 1839. It was adopted as the state flag after Texas became part of the U.S. The "lone star" is thought to represent unity. The flag remains one of the best-known in the world.

10. REPUBLIC OF THE RIO GRANDE FLAG

The Mexican states of Coahuila, Nuevo León, and Tamaulipas declared independence from the Mexican government and formed the Republic of the Rio Grande. Their flag featured a star for each of the three states. Texians volunteered to fight for the republic, which was defeated by Mexico in 1840.

11. CONFEDERATE FIRST NATIONAL FLAG

Texas joined six southern states that split from the U.S. to form the Confederate States of America (later joined by other states). The first flag of the Confederacy was the "Stars and Bars" design, but it was replaced with a flag that incorporated the better-known Battle Flag design.

12. CONFEDERATE SECOND NATIONAL FLAG

The first flag of the Confederacy so closely resembled the U.S. flag that it caused confusion on the battlefield. A new flag was adopted—named the "Stainless Banner"—which included the famous "Southern Cross" Confederate battle flag in its upper left corner.

13. CONFEDERATE THIRD NATIONAL FLAG

The second national flag also had problems, as its large white background could be mistaken for a white flag of surrender. At sea, it could also be confused with the British Royal Navy's flag, named the White Ensign. A red stripe was added, but few of these flags were made before the Confederacy surrendered.

14. UNITED STATES FLAG, 28-STARS

When Texas became a state, a 28th star was added to the U.S. flag. Texas flew the flag after the Republic of Texas ended, took it down during the Civil War, and then raised it again after the war ended. The "Stars and Stripes" flag has flown there ever since and now has 50 stars representing the states.

GOVERNMENT OF TEXAS

The government of Texas works under the Constitution of 1876. It is the state's sixth constitution since its independence from Mexico in 1836. It contains a Bill of Rights that declares Texas a free and independent state, subject only to the U.S. Constitution. Some provisions can be traced to early Spanish and Mexican roots, such as laws governing land and water rights. Hundreds of amendments have been added to the Texas Constitution since its adoption.

1888
A NEW state capitol building in Austin replaces one destroyed by fire. Taller than the U.S. capitol building in Washington, D.C., the dome has a Goddess of Liberty statue perched on top. To pay for the construction, the government sells 3 million acres of public land that becomes the XIT Ranch—once one of the world's largest.

1899
PIANIST Scott Joplin is the "King of Ragtime"—a popular style of music—after publishing "Maple Leaf Rag." Joplin, who grows up in Texarkana, writes "Treemonisha"—one of the first operas by an African American composer. He is awarded a Pulitzer Prize after his death, and inspires a generation of musicians.

1901
OIL! At Spindletop, near Beaumont, a gusher shoots oil—"black gold!"—100 feet into the air. On land explored by Pattillo Higgins and drilled by Anthony F. Lucas, the well spouts 100,000 barrels of crude oil a day for nine days before it is capped. "Wildcatters" rush to Texas, and the oil boom begins.

1915
TO CONQUER the and benefit ran farmers' lives, T improved windm water from bene ground. This all move into new state claims the windmill—until Later, Texas will farms to produce

...s adopts a new ...ution, the sixth since its ...endence from Mexico ...e one still in use today. It ...overnment power and ...ng, and establishes ...l sessions of the state ...ture. It creates the ...sity of Texas, and ...ms what is today Texas University.

1891
"JIM CROW" laws segregate white people and African Americans. For decades, African Americans in Texas are forced to use separate public facilities, attend separate schools, one pictured right, and sit in separate railroad cars. Mexican Americans face similar injustices.

1907
JEWISH immigrants arrive in Texas, some via New Mexico, while others escape attacks in Russia and Eastern Europe. Rabbi Henry Cohen leads the Galveston Movement, which settles 10,000 Jews in America. After World War II, Jewish people in Texas help Holocaust survivors move to the state.

1914
THE "GUSHER AGE" makes Texas a global oil power. The Houston Ship Channel is deepened to create a major port, first for cotton cargoes, then as a center for oil refining. Earlier, Joseph S. Cullinan forms the Texas Company— today called Texaco—to exploit Spindletop, building a pipeline to a Port Arthur refinery.

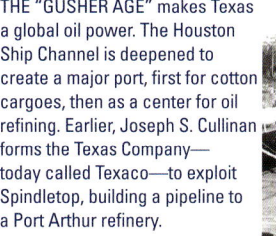

...ers kill millions of ...nvironmental ...tens the food ...ay of life of native ...e Red River War, ...ader Quanah ...arriors from other ...efeated, and his ...oved to an Indian ...ervation.

1880s — **1890s** — **1900s** — **1910s**

1876
TECHNOLOGY is changing ranching. The great cattle drives start to die out with the invention of barbed wire and later, railroad expansion. More farmers will use barbed wire to fence their property, bringing an end to the open range. But enclosing ranches leads to disputes over access to water sources and grazing land.

1900
AMERICA'S deadliest natural disaster strikes Galveston when a hurricane claims over 6,000 lives and destroys many of the port city's buildings. As part of the recovery, the city builds a protective seawall and a causeway, a raised road to the mainland. When Hotel Galvez is built in 1911, funded by locals, the city is reborn as a resort.

1910
MEXICANS seek refuge in Texas to escape the Mexican Revolution, but suffer discrimination. Tensions on the Mexican border become violent. In the turmoil, the Texas Rangers and others kill up to 5,000 Hispanic people. They face calls for reform by legislator José T. Canales, later a founder of the League of United Latin American Citizens.

...y ...tle ...ival ...e ...ps ...an,

...RS work the ...tton and other ...portion to the ...se farmers ...nslaved ...as those who ...n southern ...ed by war, and ...e. With hardly ...er, many will poverty.

1885
DR PEPPER is first produced at a Waco drugstore—back when it is also a soda shop. Store owner Wade B. Morrison hires pharmacist Charles Courtice Alderton, who experiments with soft drinks made from fruit extracts and sweeteners. One combination proves hugely popular—Dr Pepper is born.

1898
THEODORE ROOSEVELT, later a U.S. President, organizes the 1st United States Volunteer Cavalry to fight for Cuban independence from Spain. At a hotel near the Alamo in San Antonio, he recruits cowboys, outlaws, aristocrats, and college athletes, to join his legendary unit of "Rough Riders."

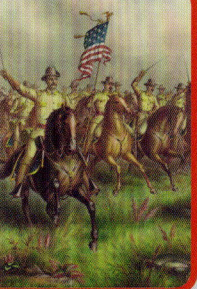

1910
JACK JOHNSON, son of a former enslaved man, is the first African American to be world heavyweight boxing champion. The "Galveston Giant" wins the title in 1908, but is not officially recognized. His title is confirmed after he defeats Jim Jeffries, a white boxer who at first refuses to fight an African American.

1914
JAMES E. FER elected Texas winning supp He pledges to of rent that la charge to tena this is ruled u Later, in 1917, abusing his p "Pa" Ferguso governor to b

19. Corpus Christi

Built during World War II, the USS *Lexington* aircraft carrier is a floating museum today. Take a self-guided tour of the flight deck to explore aircraft, including fighter jets. Head inside the ship for an exhibit about the 1941 Japanese attack on Pearl Harbor. On the city's waterfront, a life-size statue honors Tejano singer Selena. Also explore Padre Island National Seashore, a nature reserve with hundreds of bird species. In summer, visitors can watch the release of newborn turtles on a nesting beach.

20. Spindletop-Gladys City Boomtown, Beaumont

The discovery of a gigantic oil "gusher" at Spindletop changed Texas—and the world—forever. The museum recaptures the "Gusher Age" in a recreated town from the early 20th century. Pattillo Higgins, who first explored the land at Spindletop, had a vision for Gladys City, which was to have factories, homes, and parks. Visitors can step back in time to the boomtown days of oil.

21. Caddo Mounds State Historic Site, near Nacogdoches

More than 1,200 years ago, a group of Caddo people built a village west of Nacogdoches. Caddos arrived in Texas as hunter-gatherers but later turned to farming crops. Visitors can explore the everyday lives of this ancient people, whose complex culture included beautiful pottery as well as large mounds made of earth used for ceremonies.

22. Fannin Battleground State Historic Site, near Victoria, and Presidio de la Bahía, Goliad

During the Texas Revolution, Col. James W. Fannin surrendered to Mexican forces at the Battle of Coleto. Fannin and his men were later executed on the orders of Mexican military dictator Santa Anna. View the spot where Fannin surrendered, then travel to nearby Goliad to see the presidio where many executions took place.

23. Eisenhower Birthplace State Historic Site, Denison

Dwight D. Eisenhower, the 34th U.S. President, grew up in Kansas but was born at this house in Texas. Antique furniture fills the modest house, highlighting the humble life of the Eisenhowers. Thirty miles away is Bonham—the hometown of Sam Rayburn, the longest-serving Speaker of the U.S. House of Representatives. Visitors can walk in his family's footsteps in the Sam Rayburn House Museum.

24. George H. W. Bush Presidential Library and Museum, College Station

Located at Texas A&M University, the museum presents the life of George H. W. Bush, the 41st U.S. President and father of 43rd President George W. Bush. Exhibits include a restored World War II warplane, a presidential limousine, and a section of the Berlin Wall, which fell during his presidency. There's even a replica of First Lady Barbara Bush's wedding dress. Be sure to have your photo taken in a recreation of the White House Oval Office!

25. Varner-Hogg Plantation State Historic Site, West Columbia

The elegant mansion that crowns the property was built by sugarcane tycoon Columbus R. Patton in the 1830s. A tour of the house and grounds reveals life on a 19th-century sugar plantation and the hard labor of the enslaved people who worked the land.

26. Panhandle-Plains Historical Museum, Canyon, near Amarillo

From bison hunters and chuck-wagon culture to modern automobiles and fashion, this fascinating museum tells the story of "people of the Plains." As well as fossil collections, there are impressive displays of giant crocodile-like and salamander-like creatures from the time when the Texas Panhandle was a swampy, tropical rainforest. Nearby is Palo Duro Canyon, America's second largest canyon, which members of the Coronado expedition are said to have come upon during their fruitless search for gold in the 1540s.

27. Nearly 18,000 historical markers are sprinkled across Texas, with a presence in all 254 counties

These Texas Historical Commission markers identify fascinating—even spooky—sites, including everything from historic houses and public buildings to military sites and important people. Among the best-known markers are those for the Alamo and President John F. Kennedy's assassination. But creepier spots are the Austin Moonlight Towers, the Marfa Lights, above, and the Aurora Cemetery (which is said to include the grave of a UFO pilot!).

10. San Antonio River Walk

This historic walk through downtown **San Antonio** and beyond is a Texas treasure. Designed by Robert H. H. Hugman, the project kicked off in 1939. The River Walk came to life during HemisFair—the 1968 World's Fair—and played a part in the city's tricentennial celebrations in 2018. En route, relive the Old West at the Briscoe Western Art Museum. The nearby Institute of Texan Cultures highlights the state's many ethnic groups. Every April, the city's Fiesta hosts Latino music, stages a Battle of Flowers parade, and crowns its "Queen of the Order of the Alamo."

11. The Sixth Floor Museum at Dealey Plaza

Peer out of the sixth-floor **Dallas** window where Lee Harvey Oswald is said to have fired his gun at President John F. Kennedy's motorcade on the street below, assassinating the president and changing history. Located inside the former Texas School Book Depository, the museum features a timeline of JFK's life. The sniper's perch in the window has been recreated based on crime scene photography from November 22, 1963—the day the president was shot.

12. George W. Bush Presidential Library and Museum

Located on the **Dallas** campus of Southern Methodist University, the museum honors the presidency of George W. Bush. Experience life inside the White House, and learn about the president's response to the September 11 terrorist attacks. Stop at the African American Museum, Dallas, to experience the nation's largest African American folk art collection.

13. Fort Worth Stockyards National Historic District

Once populated by cowboys and cattlemen, the Stockyards are among the most popular attractions in Texas. Moo-ve on over to the twice-daily cattle drive of the Fort Worth Herd or check out the Stockyards Championship Rodeo. The Fort Worth Museum of Science and History also has an excellent dinosaur exhibit. Visit the city's Kimbell Art Museum to view over 350 works from around the world.

14. Big Bend National Park

This West Texas park covers part of the Chihuahuan Desert and is known for its dinosaur and mammoth fossil beds. From there, drive to Seminole Canyon State Park and Historic Site, famous for its rock art. Guadalupe Mountains National Park, also in West Texas, is home to the state's highest point, and the towering rock formation El Capitan. Take a day trip to Fort Davis National Historic Site, where "Buffalo Soldiers" were stationed.

15. Galveston

This long-established coastal city, which spans Galveston Island and Pelican Island, includes the Historic Downtown Strand Seaport district, the Pleasure Pier, above, and Moody Gardens with its Aquarium Pyramid. The Ocean Star Drilling Rig Museum offers tours of an oil rig, while the Galveston Railroad Museum has a large restored collection. The city's star attraction is the Galveston Seawall, a major engineering feat constructed to prevent flooding after the devastating hurricane of 1900. Birthplace of "Juneteenth," an Emancipation Proclamation Reading takes place in Galveston each year.

16. El Paso

The El Paso Mission Trail includes two mission churches—Ysleta and Socorro, above—and the nearby presidio chapel of San Elizario, symbols of a rich history that embraces Spain, Mexico, and the U.S. Ysleta was built by Tigua Indians, a Pueblo tribe still in Texas. A museum within the Tigua Indian Cultural Center highlights their history and traditions. Visit the University of Texas at El Paso for one of America's most unusual architectural sights—buildings inspired by the Himalayan kingdom of Bhutan.

17. Fredericksburg

Founded by German colonists in 1846, the city began as a German-Texas settlement known for making peace with the Comanches. Today, Main Street is a living museum. Discover the Vereins Kirche, above—a replica of the settlers' first public building—and the National Museum of the Pacific War, which tells the dramatic history of World War II in the Pacific. Visit the nearby Texas Rangers Heritage Center and Fort Martin Scott, a fascinating restoration of an early U.S. military post. The massive dome of Enchanted Rock is about 20 miles away.

18. Waco

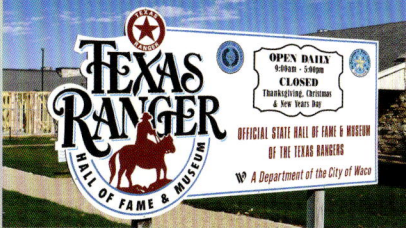

The Texas Ranger Hall of Fame and Museum displays 14,000 artifacts, including firearms and badges, and also honors Rangers who died in service. Nearby is the Dr Pepper Museum for fans of the soft drink. At the Waco Mammoth National Monument, view fossils of the only nursery herd of Columbian mammoths so far discovered in the U.S. You can walk in the tracks of dinosaurs at nearby Dinosaur Valley State Park.

e dry climate
chers' and
exas uses
hills to pump
eath the
ows settlers to
areas. The
world's tallest
t blows over.
use wind
electricity.

WORLD WAR I

THE U.S. abandons neutrality and joins this global conflict in 1917, declaring war on the German Empire after public outrage at American deaths from submarine warfare. More than a million U.S. soldiers are sent to the Western Front in Europe to help fight against the final German offensive. Germany is defeated, and the U.S. emerges as a world power.

1924

MIRIAM "MA" FERGUSON is elected as Texas' first female governor. She is the wife of impeached governor James "Pa" Ferguson and faces criticism for being controlled by him. In the Prohibition era, "Ma" opposes the ban on sales of alcoholic beverages and clashes with Texas Rangers over alleged corruption.

PROHIBITION

THE 18th Amendment to the U.S. Constitution bans the sale of alcoholic beverages in an attempt to curb crime and poverty. It is championed by U.S. Senator from Texas Morris Sheppard, named the "father of national Prohibition." Federal agents try to enforce the ban, but crime gangs and "bootleggers" make fortunes from illegal alcohol sales. The 21st Amendment ends Prohibition in 1933.

1941

TEXAS is one of the largest military training grounds in World War II, and the state's oil fuels the U.S. military effort. Its army bases and airfields train more than a million people. A shortage of male pilots leads to the creation of a base at Sweetwater to train female pilots, nicknamed WASPs.

1936

AS THE Great Depression wears on, Texas celebrates 100 years of independence. To advertise itself to the world, a $25-million Centennial Exposition is held in Dallas. Six million people attend, including President Franklin D. Roosevelt. In 1968, San Antonio marks its 250th anniversary with a similar event, called HemisFair '68.

1919

TEXAS becomes the first in the South to approve the 19th Amendment to the U.S. Constitution, giving women the right to vote in national and state elections. It is a triumph for groups that fought for women's rights, such as the Texas Equal Suffrage Association, led by Minnie Fisher Cunningham of Galveston.

1929

THE LEAGUE of United Latin American Citizens becomes the first national Mexican-American civil rights organization, formed in Corpus Christi. It follows the First Mexican Congress, held in Laredo in 1911. After World War II, the American G.I. Forum, also formed in Corpus Christi, will provide a voice for Mexican Americans.

1920s   **1930s**   **1940s**

1917

TEXANS support U.S. entry into World War I after the Zimmermann Telegram reveals a German plot to help Mexico take back lands "stolen" by America. Some 200,000 Texans, including 450 women in the Nurse Corps, serve during the war. Texas has many training bases, including ones for recently invented airplanes.

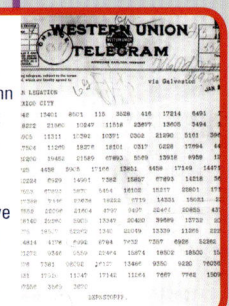

WOMEN'S SUFFRAGE

IN 1920, the 19th Amendment to the U.S. Constitution gives women the vote in national elections. Women's rights become a national issue after the 1848 Seneca Falls Convention. But World War I is the turning point for women's suffrage. With men fighting overseas, women fill jobs often held by men. After the war—with the National American Woman Suffrage Association leading the campaign—women finally win the right to vote.

1934

FORMER Texas Ranger Frank Hamer tracks down infamous outlaws Bonnie Parker and Clyde Barrow. Tales of their bank robberies and murders enthrall many during the Depression era. The villains are slain in a surprise attack. The U.S. Congress gives Hamer a special award, and the Rangers' reputation is restored.

1945

OF 750,
armed
33 are
Honor.
Mess a
fires on
his shi
Harb
of the
soldie

GUSON is
governor after
rt from the poor.
limit the amount
downers can
nt farmers. But
constitutional.
he is accused of
wers of office.
is the only Texas
impeached.

1918

AFTER years of campaigning by **suffragists**, Texas Governor William P. Hobby passes a law allowing women to vote in **primary elections.** Annie Webb Blanton becomes the first woman elected to statewide office in Texas. She oversees the state's schools as superintendent of public instruction.

1935

LACK of rain, high winds, and poor farming practices create the "Dust Bowl," turning parts of Texas into a desert. Amarillo has blinding storms between January and March, including one blackout lasting 11 hours. Crops are ruined, and many farmers head west along Route 66—one of America's first highways.

THE NEW

In 1933, President
"New Deal" helps pu
back to work after
Depression—the wo
slump in modern tim
is elected after a l
vote in the South
Texas. The New De
employment projects
social welfare, an
programs, creating
for those ha

1921

TEXAS-BORN Bessie Coleman gains her pilot's license in France, after being barred from U.S. flying schools because of her race. Of African American and Native American descent, she is the first woman pilot from either group. She goes on to thrill crowds as a daredevil stunt flyer, but dies in a plane accident in 1926.

1948
A CATTLE drive on the Chisholm Trail is retold in *Red River*. More movies about Texas follow, including *Giant*, a story of oil riches and enemies, starring James Dean. On TV and in film, the *Lone Ranger*—Texas Ranger turned masked man—fights outlaws with his Native American friend Tonto.

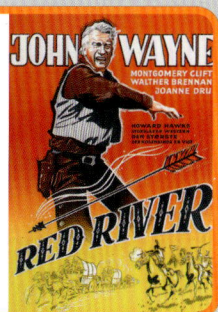

1956
HENRY B. GONZALEZ of San Antonio, a civil rights activist, becomes the first Tejano in the 20th century to win a seat in the Texas Senate. Later, he is elected to the U.S. House of Representatives. In the 1980s, Henry Cisneros is mayor of San Antonio, the city's first Latino mayor since the 1840s.

CIVIL RIGHTS MOVEMENT
After Rosa Parks refuses to vacate her bus seat for a white person in 1955, the Civil Rights Movement gains momentum. Martin Luther King, Jr. later makes a speech about his dream in which all people are treated equally. He is assassinated in 1968. In Texas, an influential 1966 march on Austin draws attention to the plight of Mexican-American farmworkers.

1969
SURGEON Denton [ ] the first to implant [ ] artificial heart in a [ ] The male patient li[ ] 64 hours. Cooley p[ ] 5,000 heart operati[ ] including 17 transp[ ] the age of 50. He f[ ] Texas Heart Institu[ ] Houston, one of A[ ] top medical center[ ]

WORLD WAR II
THE U.S. enters World War II in 1941 when Japan bombs Pearl Harbor, a U.S. naval base in Hawaii. Some 16 million serve in the American Armed Forces: 400,000 die. In 1945, the U.S. becomes the world's first superpower when Nazi Germany is defeated, and Japan surrenders after atom bombs are dropped on Hiroshima and Nagasaki.

1953
DWIGHT D. EISENHOWER, who was born in Denison, is elected as the 34th U.S. President and serves for two terms. Eisenhower is admired for his success as Supreme Commander of the 1944 D-Day invasion in World War II, and is praised for handling the Soviet Union during the Cold War and nuclear age.

1959
BUDDY HOLLY, born in Lubbock as Charles Hardin Holley, is one of the first rock 'n' roll stars. He records a string of hits, and his music influences legends such as Bob Dylan and The Beatles. While on tour, Holly's plane crashes, killing him and other musicians on board, including Texas-born The Big Bopper. Holly is only 22.

1963
HOURS after President Kennedy's tragic assassination in Dallas, Vice President Lyndon B. Johnson is sworn in as 36th U.S. President. Texas-born "LBJ" passes laws that try to end segregation and protect African Americans' right to vote. He seeks to improve healthcare and education, but the Vietnam War casts a shadow.

1950s

1960s

[ ] Texans in the U.S. [ ]ervices in World War II, [ ]awarded the Medal of [ ]Texas war heroes include [ ]ttendant Doris Miller, who [ ]p is attacked at Pearl [ ]r, and Audie Murphy, one [ ]most decorated combat [ ]rs in U.S. history.

1952
CYD CHARISSE, born in Amarillo, overcomes polio to become one of Hollywood's most celebrated dancers. She pairs with performers Fred Astaire and Gene Kelly. Kelly chooses her for the memorable "Broadway Melody" ballet in *Singin' in the Rain*. Dancer Ginger Rogers is another movie great who grows up for a time in Texas.

THE COLD WAR
The U.S. and its Allies form NATO in 1949, an organization set up to strengthen power against the Soviet Union, following years of tension after World War II. Decades of nuclear-armed stand-off begin, with Western and Eastern Europe divided by the "Iron Curtain." The world narrowly escapes nuclear war when Russia plans to base missiles in Cuba, and America will fight costly wars in Korea and—amid popular protests—Vietnam. The Cold War ends with the Soviet Union's collapse in 1991.

1967
LAWYER Barbara Jordan, bor[ ] Houston, is elected to the Tex[ ] Senate. She is the first Africa[ ] American state senator since [ ] 1880s. Later, she will become [ ] first African American woman [ ] from a southern state to serve [ ] the U.S. Congress. She will ga[ ] nationwide respect for her ro[ ] the **Watergate** hearings.

1950
BABE DIDRIKSON ZAHARIAS—born in Port Arthur to Norwegian parents—is named "Woman Athlete of the Half Century." She becomes a role model after winning two gold medals in track-and-field at the 1932 Los Angeles Olympics. She turns to golf, winning many Ladies Professional Golf Association championships.

1950
CIVIL RIGHTS begin to take center stage. African American student Heman Marion Sweatt challenges the University of Texas School of Law when it refuses to accept him. His case goes to the **U.S. Supreme Court**, which orders the end of segregated professional schools, helping end segregation in education.

[ ]DEAL

[ ]Roosevelt's [ ]t Americans [ ]r the Great [ ]rst economic [ ]s. Roosevelt [ ]uge popular [ ], including [ ]al launches [ ], experimental [ ]d insurance [ ] jobs and relief [ ]dest hit.

1958
ENGINEER Jack Kilby of Dallas-based Texas Instruments invents the "integrated circuit." It will change the technology industry forever. Later, the microchip will provide the "brains" for the company's handheld calculator. In 2000, Kilby, pictured as an older man, receives the Nobel Prize in Physics.

1969
"HOUSTON" is the historic [ ] word spoken from the Moo[ ] surface when Apollo 11's [ ] Armstrong informs Missio[ ] Control in Houston of the fi[ ] human lunar landing. The [ ] landing and return achieve[ ] a goal set by President Kennedy—which he announced at Houston's R[ ] University in 1962.

PLACES TO VISIT

1. Texas State Capitol

Take a free tour of this amazing building in **Austin** to learn about Texas history and lawmaking. See the towering central dome, a giant portrait of David Crockett, and a painting of Mexican military dictator Santa Anna's surrender at the Battle of San Jacinto. The impressive grounds feature the Tejano Monument, the Texas African American History Memorial, and the Heroes of the Alamo Monument. Nearby, the original General Land Office—Austin's oldest state building—houses the Texas Capitol Visitors Center.

2. Bullock Texas State History Museum

Witness more than 16,000 years of Texas history at the state's official history museum in **Austin**. Explore civilizations found in Texas before the arrival of Europeans. View *La Belle*, the 300-year-old shipwrecked vessel of French explorer René Robert Cavelier, Sieur de La Salle. Original artifacts tell the stories of the Texas Revolution, the Civil War, ranching, oil, civil rights, and more, celebrating the roles of diverse people making their mark on Texas history.

3. LBJ Presidential Library

This **Austin** museum records the life and times of Texan Lyndon Baines Johnson, 36th U.S. President, and his wife, Claudia Taylor "Lady Bird" Johnson. Located within the University of Texas at Austin, the library has 45 million pages of historical documents as well as exhibits covering the Civil Rights Movement and Vietnam War.

4. Texas State Library and Archives Commission

While there have been an official library and archives since the days of the Texas Republic, the agency was officially formed in 1909. The present building, completed in the 1960s, is located next to **Austin**'s state capitol. Named for Lorenzo de Zavala—who briefly served as Vice President of the Texas Republic and helped write its constitution—the building houses state archives, a library, and a genealogy collection. Check out more online, including Texas maps dating from the 18th century, historical state flags, and William B. Travis' famous Alamo letter of 1836.

5. Ann W. Richards Congress Avenue Bridge

Prepare to be amazed by one of the world's biggest urban bat colonies. After dusk, from April to October, watch up to 1.5 million free-tailed bats fly from under this **Austin** bridge. A riverboat cruise on Lady Bird Lake gets you even closer to the action. Wander down Congress Avenue to the Mexic-Arte Museum, which exhibits Latino art and culture, or splash around in Barton Springs.

6. Space Center Houston

This world-class attraction in **Houston** features over 400 space artifacts, including Moon rock, a life-size Skylab Trainer, and the Apollo 17 Command Module flown by Eugene Cernan—the last person to walk on the Moon. See a replica of the space shuttle *Independence* and explore the future of travel to Mars. Take a tram through the NASA Johnson Space Center and visit Historic Mission Control. Rocket Park is also home to a gigantic restored Saturn V rocket.

7. San Jacinto Battleground State Historic Site

Located near **Houston**, this 1,200-acre park features the towering San Jacinto Monument and the San Jacinto Museum of History. On this site in 1836, Sam Houston led the Texas Army to victory over Mexican military dictator Santa Anna's forces and secured Texas independence. The monument's observation deck offers a bird's-eye view of the battleground. Head down to the water to visit the battleship USS *Texas*, now retired, the only surviving U.S. Navy warship to serve in both World Wars, and a National Historic Landmark.

8. The Houston Museum of Natural Science

Feast your eyes on prehistoric beasts in the **Houston** museum's Morian Hall of Paleontology, then gaze at the stars in the planetarium. Close to downtown is the Buffalo Soldiers National Museum, dedicated to the African Americans who served in the U.S. Armed Forces after the Civil War. Many were formerly enslaved, protecting settlers, stagecoaches, and cattle herds on the western frontier against raids by Native American people.

9. The Alamo and San Antonio Missions National Historical Park

Remember the Alamo! The former Catholic mission entered history when Texas defenders fought to the death against Mexican forces. Today, the **San Antonio** complex includes a church and Long Barrack Museum. Nearby, explore El Camino Real de los Tejas, the original "royal road" made a National Historic Trail in 2004. It linked Spanish missions, including others in San Antonio that can still be seen. With the Alamo, they form a UNESCO World Heritage Site.

MAP OF TEXAS AND PLACES TO VISIT

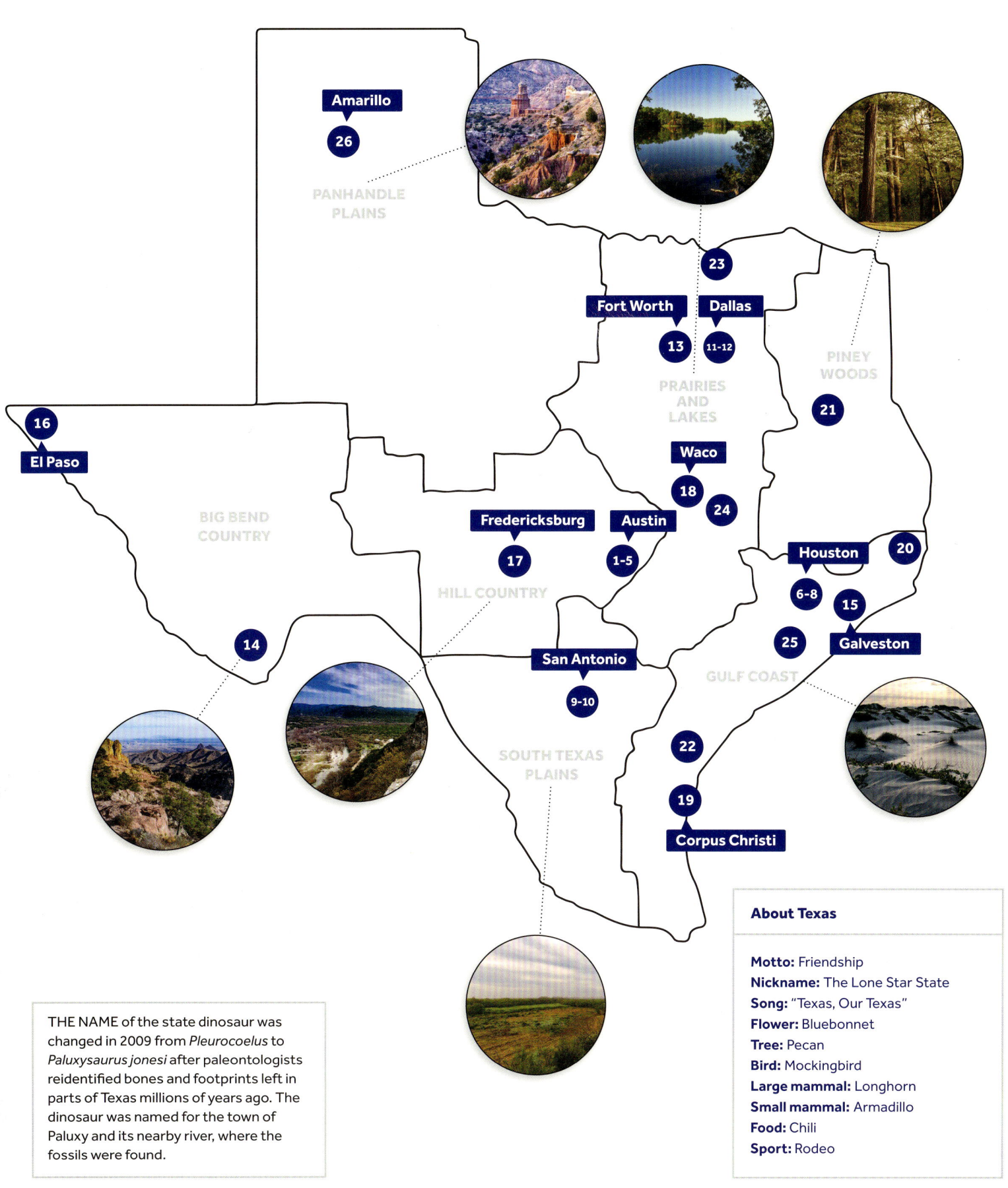

Amarillo
26

PANHANDLE PLAINS

23

Fort Worth
13

Dallas
11-12

PINEY WOODS

PRAIRIES AND LAKES

El Paso
16

BIG BEND COUNTRY

Fredericksburg
17

Austin
1-5

Waco
18
24

Houston
6-8

20

15

Galveston

HILL COUNTRY

14

25

San Antonio
9-10

GULF COAST

SOUTH TEXAS PLAINS

22

19

Corpus Christi

About Texas

Motto: Friendship
Nickname: The Lone Star State
Song: "Texas, Our Texas"
Flower: Bluebonnet
Tree: Pecan
Bird: Mockingbird
Large mammal: Longhorn
Small mammal: Armadillo
Food: Chili
Sport: Rodeo

THE NAME of the state dinosaur was changed in 2009 from *Pleurocoelus* to *Paluxysaurus jonesi* after paleontologists reidentified bones and footprints left in parts of Texas millions of years ago. The dinosaur was named for the town of Paluxy and its nearby river, where the fossils were found.

1981
MISSION CONTROL in Houston directs the flight of Space Shuttle *Columbia*. After its two flights, it becomes the first spacecraft to be reused. Space shuttles, pictured right, fly more than 350 people during 135 missions controlled from Houston, though two disasters claim 14 lives.

2009
BEYONCÉ, born in Houston, is named *Billboard*'s Top Female Artist of the decade and later is in *Time* magazine's list of the 100 most influential people in the world. Selling millions of records, she describes herself a "modern-day feminist," and performs at presidential inauguration events for Barack Obama.

ASSASSINATION OF KENNEDY

JOHN F. KENNEDY, the popular 35th U.S. President, is shot while traveling in a Dallas motorcade on November 22, 1963, and dies of his wounds. The nation is horrified and grief-stricken. Lee Harvey Oswald is said to have fired the shots that killed the president. Oswald is murdered by Texas nightclub owner Jack Ruby before he can face trial.

1995
SELENA, a Mexican American born in Lake Jackson, is "Queen of Tejano Music." She is one of the most successful Latina artists of all time. At first, some people refuse to let Selena perform because she sings traditionally male-dominated Tejano music. But her popularity grows. She is killed by a former employee.

2000
TEXAS Governor George W. Bush—son of President George H. W. Bush—is elected 43rd U.S. President. Following terrorist attacks in 2001, Bush declares a "war on terror," and U.S. military operations abroad begin. His administration is known for its landmark education programs.

2017
THE HOUSTON ASTROS baseball team wins the World Series, a first for the team—and for Texas! Houston celebrates with a victory parade attended by thousands of fans. The Astrodome, the Astros' former home and the world's first multi-purpose domed sports stadium, is set to be renovated as an events space.

1970s **1980s** **1990s** **2000s** **2010s**

1974
THE MUSIC program *Austin City Limits* airs in front of a live audience. It becomes the longest-running music program in U.S. television history. The show features many musical styles and performances by stars, including Willie Nelson and George Jones. Austin is later known as the "Live Music Capital of the World."

AUSTIN CITY LIMITS®

2014
THE SAN ANTONIO SPURS win their fifth NBA championship—one of the greatest runs in modern basketball history. Their rivalry with the Los Angeles Lakers is famous, the two teams having met in the playoffs many times. Star players include Tim Duncan, right, and, earlier, David "The Admiral" Robinson.

1972
TEXAS is football. The Dallas Cowboys win Super Bowl VI, the first of five world championships. They dominate the game in the 1970s and 1990s, and are tagged "America's Team" due to their national popularity. Troy Aikman, Roger Staubach, and Emmitt Smith are among the Cowboys' greatest stars.

1988
TEXAS oil millionaire and World War II navy pilot, George H. W. Bush is elected 41st U.S. President. The Soviet Union collapses while he is in office. He launches an attack on Iraq after the country invades oil-rich Kuwait. Bush also negotiates an agreement to improve trade between the U.S., Canada, and Mexico.

2000
MICHAEL "SUPERMAN" JOHNSON—who was born in Dallas and attended Baylor University—wins gold at the Sydney Olympics. At the 1996 Atlanta Olympics, Johnson becomes the first man to win both the 200- and 400-meter events. He is one of the world's greatest track-and-field athletes.

2019
THE "TEXAS MYSTIQUE" lives on. The state is America's second most populous, after California, with about 29 million people. It has one of the world's largest economies and is a leader in U.S. exports. The Lone Star State has a unique heritage, and is home to people from many different cultures and backgrounds.